PERSONAL SELF INTEGRATION:

Introduction to Basic Selves

HARVEY TYLER GRADY, D.D.

PERSONAL SELF INTEGRATION: INTRODUCTION TO BASIC SELVES

iUniverse books may be ordered through booksellers or by contacting:

iUniverse
1663 Liberty Drive
Bloomington, IN 47403
www.iuniverse.com
844-349-9409

Because of the dynamic nature of the Internet, any web addresses or links contained in this book may have changed since publication and may no longer be valid. The views expressed in this work are solely those of the author and do not necessarily reflect the views of the publisher, and the publisher hereby disclaims any responsibility for them.

Any people depicted in stock imagery provided by Getty Images are models, and such images are being used for illustrative purposes only. Certain stock imagery © Getty Images.

ISBN: 978-1-6632-4487-1 (sc)
ISBN: 978-1-6632-4488-8 (e)

Print information available on the last page.

iUniverse rev. date: 11/02/2022

APPRECIATION

I wish to thank all the wonderful people who have contributed to this booklet through sharing their experiences with Basic Selves. Special thanks go to my wife, Julie, for her invaluable support and assistance. I am deeply thankful for the pioneering work by Wayne Guthrie and Bella Karish, founders of the Fellowship of Universal Guidance. Their dedication and clarity have opened new (and ancient) dimensions of human experience that benefit us all.

TRAINING AVAILABLE

Persons interested in Personal Self Integration may enroll in training programs on two levels:

1. *as trainees learning Self-help skills; or*
2. *as therapists learning individual and group therapeutic skills for certification by the Center for Human Potential.*

HARVEY AND JULIE GRADY

Raised on cattle ranches in the Arizona countryside, Harvey has always been curious about the inner workings of people and nature. In college he studied both sciences and humanities. His professional career spans highway safety analysis, social work, justice system planning, the corrections system, prevention of juvenile delinquency, behavioral health, food system planning, and roles as therapist, educator, and researcher in energy medicine. Sixty years of experience in community projects and counseling individuals, families, and groups, give his work a practical flavor. His interest lies in empowering people to solve their problems and realize their potentials.

Julie Jerrell Grady adds her exquisite artistic skills to the creative adventure the Gradys call "Personal Self Integration." Born in Phoenix and raised in several states as her family traveled, Julie became a visual artist whose paintings convey a sparkling vitality. Her counseling skills have helped clients discover their Inner Selves and learn how to embrace their inner powers and potentials.

CONTENTS

LIST OF FIGURES

ACHIEVING HUMAN POTENTIAL

When we seek help for resolving troubles or personal betterment, we often discover how to expand our human potential. We learn to tap inner resources that lie beyond our normal abilities. By expanding our capabilities, we gain insights and skills for solving problems. We also learn how to live more fulfilling and meaningful lives.

This booklet presents part of the Personal Self Integration system for assisting us to reach our human potential. Personal Self Integration (PSI) skills help us discover and integrate the Inner Selves that provide or block *access* to the valuable inner resources we all have. We are blocked from utilizing our talents to the greatest extent or from living our lives to the fullest. We get bogged down in problems instead of expressing our positive potential. Too often we get stuck in a state of powerlessness, too heavy with inertia to progress, instead of using our personal power to help our Selves grow.

When we are faced with persistent problems, our perspective is often too limited to allow solutions. Our perspective *can* expand, giving us access to previously hidden, underlying causes of the problem. We *can* perceive options that we did not previously recognize, and we *can* learn skills for exercising those options. Through this training process, we learn *how* to transform our Selves.

Transforming our Selves implies that we can gain greater awareness, acceptance and love of our Selves and others. We need to be aware of those parts of our personality that function well, giving us *strength*, and those that don't function well, giving us *weakness*. But we might have difficulty in being objectively aware of our Selves. Our own biases, prejudices, and blind spots hamper objectivity. We need ways to identify and overcome these obstacles to objectivity so that we can be truly aware of our personality's assets and liabilities.

To become more accepting and loving of our Selves, we need to know our Selves more fully. Great teachers have advised: **Know thy Self!** How can this be done? With the evolution of psychology, several methods are now available for knowing our Selves more fully. Freud[1] identified the *conscious* and *sub*conscious minds. Jung[2], Assagioli[3], Maslow[4] and others[5][6] identified and began to explore the *super*conscious mind. The emerging picture of the human mind is shown as a field of consciousness with at least three levels (see Fig. 1).

Personal Self Integration provides us with an easy way to become "friends" with our subconscious mind, and even beyond that, our superconscious mind.

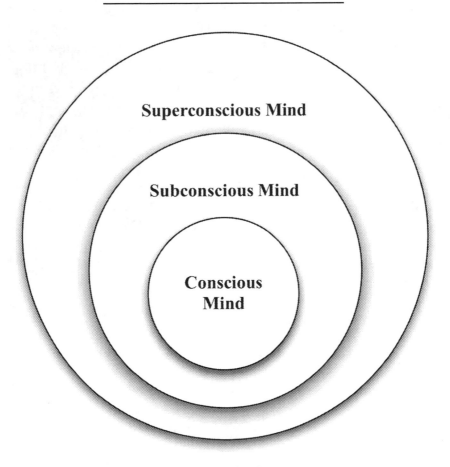

Superconscious Mind

Subconscious Mind

Conscious Mind

Figure 1. Three Levels of Consciousness

We can now think of the achievement of human potential as expanding the scope of our consciousness from the limited range of the conscious mind into the broader ranges of the subconscious and superconscious levels of mind. How can we do this?

When we try to "meet" our subconscious mind, we can easily feel overwhelmed. Although hundreds of books have been written on this subject, contact with the subconscious mind remains a mysterious and formidable challenge for most people. An introduction to our subconscious mind may seem as difficult as having a two-way conversation with the ocean, so a more "friendly" approach would be helpful. Personal Self Integration provides us with an easy way to become "friends" with our subconscious mind, and even beyond that, with our superconscious mind.

The research of Drs. Wayne Guthrie and Bella Karish yields a framework for accessing subconscious and superconscious levels of mind. Their books, [7]*Pathways to Your Three Selves [1989]*, [8]*Working with Your Three Selves [2005]*, [9]*Portals to Your Higher Consciousness [2017]*, describe their discoveries of Basic Selves and High Selves through thirty years of psychic counseling. Several terms used in Personal Self Integration to identify specific aspects of the levels of mind, such as *Basic Self* and *High Self*, are derived from their work. Because Personal Self Integration has developed as a separate, yet related system of personal growth, these terms sometimes vary from definitions given by Guthrie and Karish.

Their method involved psychic counseling in which Karish channeled a Basic Self or a High Self for the person being counseled while Guthrie questioned that Self to obtain its view of a problem or opportunity. In contrast, Personal Self Integration allows a person seeking growth the opportunity of conducting their own dialogue with their Basic Selves and High Self. The Personal Self Integration system adapts the conceptual framework of Drs. Guthrie and Karish to focus on the *process of personal empowerment* through acquisition of inner awareness, communication, and transformational skills.

Personal Self Integration calls the conscious mind the "Outer Self." This term assists in correcting a possible misconception that *only* the conscious mind possesses the attributes of Self awareness, choice, history, and independence of action. The term "Outer Self" refers to the aspect of the personality that focuses attention on the outer physical world, while its subconscious and superconscious aspects focus attention on other levels of life that are just as or more valid as physical life.

Personal Self Integration quickly reveals an *Outer Self bias* – that it is the only aspect of the personality that exercises choice and expresses values and abilities. Philosophers, scientists, and spiritual authorities have long recognized the difference between a person's *voluntary* and *involuntary* reactions and behaviors. They have noted that a person's intentions are often confused and engaged in conflict. Personal Self Integration sheds light on this important fact and offers *more precise* distinctions that support a person's ability to resolve conflicting reactions, behaviors, and intentions.

In the Personal Self Integration process of meeting and befriending Inner Selves, a person rapidly learns that her/his Outer Self's intentions often do *not* jibe with Basic Self or High Self intentions. However, when an Outer Self identifies the differences between its intentions and an Inner Self's intentions, it gains an understanding that leads to achieving an inner compromise that resolves the conflict. That capability empowers the Outer Self to address seemingly impossible challenges and develop greater skill in solving problems that arise in inner and outer experiences.

Our experience of more than thirty years and thousands of clients provides tangible evidence that as we resolve our inner blocks and conflicts, our relationships with others improve accordingly. This book presents several case examples of how our clients have used Personal Self Integration tools to improve their lives. (See section on Case Examples)

PERSONAL SELF INTEGRATION

The Personal Self Integration concept offers a "friendly" method for us to become acquainted with our subconscious and superconscious levels of mind. In this approach, we use social skills that are already familiar – skills that we use in meeting other persons – for meeting "Selves" representing our subconscious and superconscious minds. (See Fig. 2) we meet our **Basic Selves** that represent the usually separated masculine and feminine aspects of our subconscious mind, and our **High Self** that represents the fully integrated masculine and feminine aspects of our superconscious mind. We are given access to deeper and higher levels of mind where we meet Inner Selves in the same way that we meet other persons.

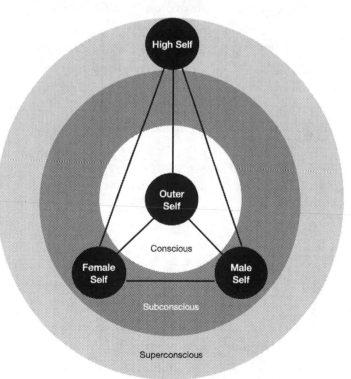

Figure 2. Outer Self, Basic Selves and High Self

The Outer Self interacts with the Basic Selves and High Self constantly, yet is unaware of those interactions. Consequently, the Outer Self might feel overpowered at times by subconscious and superconscious dynamics and not be aware that it can communicate with those Inner Selves. The lines in Figure 2 identify the lines of communication that the Outer Self can develop with Basic Selves and the High Self to dialogue with them. The Outer Self can learn how to perform this inner dialogue to achieve valuable benefits:

1. The ability to "hear" what Inner Selves say.
2. The ability to ask questions and receive responses from Inner Selves.
3. The ability to gain a more accurate understanding of Inner Self needs and be able to take action to meet those needs.
4. The ability to build mutual trust and respect with Inner Selves so they can feel safe and supported by the Outer Self.
5. The ability to ask for information from Basic Selves and especially from the High Self.
6. The ability to request specific helpful actions by Basic Selves and the High Self in supporting the personality and other personalities, such as in prayer.
7. The ability to obtain specific guidance from the High Self to assist the Outer Self in making decisions and learning karmic lessons.

We have a fundamental choice in accessing the deeper fields of consciousness of our personality. We can stay at a distance and view our subconscious and superconscious levels of mind from an external, *impersonal* position. That view gives us some understanding as we observe events in our awareness, yet it keeps us in a limited comfort zone of perception. We can easily stay stuck in a perceptual rut and lack the sensitivity and abilities that empower us to solve inner problems.

Personal Self Integration offers us techniques that take an internal, *personal* approach for developing competence in establishing communication with Inner Selves. However, this personal approach for some of us might evoke a sense of risk and move us out of our comfort zone of perception. From the experience of hundreds of clients, we can safely conclude that taking the risk produces multiple benefits that far outweigh the risk. We have found that *Personal Self* Integration offers valuable tools to persons committed to grow into their human potential.

We make a distinction between "inner" and "outer" Selves. A person has one Outer Self that relates to the outer world of physical life. It is strongly associated with the physical body. It is born when the physical body is born, and leaves the physical body at death, transitioning as a unique energetic individuality to a position among Subconscious Selves. Inner Selves exist *before* and *after* the existence of the Outer Self and maintain their existence in a nonphysical energy state. When we communicate with Inner Selves, we access a wide range of life experience beyond the physical that explains our recurrent problems and challenges.

Because modern Western cultures have emphasized "outer" aspects of experience, many Westerners think that only "external materiality" is real and objective and that "inner experience" is either unreal or subjective. Yet developments in quantum physics have shown that external experience is no more or less *real* than internal experience, just differently focused. As psychology progresses toward a more definitive, detailed wealth of knowledge that extends our physical sciences, we are provided with the opportunity to make significant "inner" discoveries.[8,9,10] Personal Self Integration offers a ready pathway for a person to discover Inner Selves that play important roles in daily living.

Personal Self Integration offers a ready pathway
for a person to discover Inner Selves
that play important roles in daily living.

Within the Personal Self Integration framework, these Inner Selves represent important aspects of our being, and they deserve proper recognition. To create "equality among Selves," a person's conscious mind is referred to as the **Outer Self**. For example, a woman named Jill is considered an "Outer Self," and we recognize her by her given name. However, her Basic Selves are called other names, such as Sally and Sam. Each Self has a name and equal standing. This recognition promotes greater acceptance and tolerance of one Self for another in an atmosphere that recognizes that *all Selves are worthy* and have their place in the "inner family" of a personality.

All Selves are worthy and have their place in the "inner family" of a personality.

We define a *Self* as a focal point of consciousness representing an aspect of a person that *contributes* to the whole personality. In this view, we find only one Self in the field of the conscious or outer mind, and we call it the "Outer Self." Many persons identify only with their Outer Self and *disown* their subconscious and superconscious aspects, unnecessarily limiting their personality.

The range of the subconscious mind appears more extensive than the range of the Outer Self, and there we discover at least two gender-based Selves that we term the "Male Self" and "Female Self." The Male and Female Selves form a crucial *base* for spiritual growth when they voluntarily merge their polarized life energies into unified, androgynous consciousness. Hence they are referred to as "Basic Selves."

In an ongoing process of discovery in our inner research, we have identified three other Subconscious Selves – Mental Judge Self, Astral Judge Self, and Body Self – and briefly characterize them here. Other books will be written to describe those Selves and their interactions in greater depth.

The Mental Judge Self most often expresses fear and doubt, judging, blaming and shaming the other Selves to maintain its safety. It often acts as a catalyst for challenging Basic Selves to grow *beyond* their judgments and limiting beliefs. Due to its intense fear, a Mental Judge Self often blocks or distorts communication between the Outer Self and Basic Selves and between Outer Self and High Self.

Figure 3 shows the Outer Self as a region of consciousness that communicates with Inner Selves occupying broader fields of consciousness. Within the focus of this book, the Mental Judge Self can be seen initially as a hindrance, while the High Self can be seen as an aid to the Outer Self in establishing communication with Basic Selves.

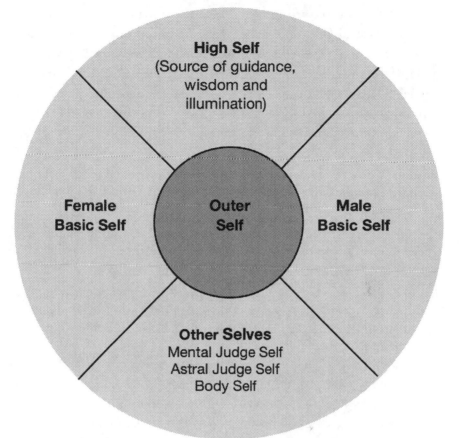

Figure 3. Personal Self Integration Format

Figure 3 shows subconscious Selves forming an environment of consciousness for the Outer Self and the High Self guiding the personality. Soul maintains the personality's individuality within universal consciousness. The Outer Self interacts and perceives the reality of universal consciousness mainly through Subconscious Selves who are caught in illusion. The High Self helps the Outer Self penetrate illusion before all the Subconscious Selves are ready and willing to penetrate illusion.

Sub-Selves

We can discover more Selves than these within the subconscious mind, such as the "inner child" or "critical parent."[4][10] A number of inner disowned Selves identified in the therapeutic system of Voice Dialogue, developed by Hal Stone and Sidra Winkelman, also speak within us at times.[11] These sub-Selves can also have value for our personal growth.

However, our research has shown that these sub-Selves represent fragmented aspects of the more enduring Male, Female, Judge and Body Selves. The "inner child" and "critical parent" of Transactional Analysis or Psychosynthesis are often tied to childhood traumas and represent only small fragments of the more substantial Subconscious Selves. Disowned Selves most often relate to specific strategies of the Mental Judge Self or to untapped potentials of Basic Selves. All Selves that choose to emerge are welcomed and included in the process of Personal Self Integration.

We view the personality as a jewel with many facets. Each facet adds to the value of the jewel by revealing a greater range of potential.

We view the personality as a jewel with many facets. Each facet adds to the value of the jewel by revealing a greater range of potential. How can we be whole beings if we do not recognize all aspects of our nature? Furthermore, most of our problems and limitations appear to come from unrecognized, blocked and needy Subconscious Selves. The expanded leadership role of the Outer Self leads to meeting and helping Subconscious Selves resolve their problems and needs in ways constructive to the entire personality.

Once we meet our Subconscious Selves and help them achieve harmony of purpose, we can reach into the field of the *superconscious* mind to meet our High Self. The High Self gives us wise, practical, and specific counsel. It also advises and assists Subconscious Selves when they also seek its guidance. Subconscious Selves have freedom to make their own decisions, independent of other Selves. Sometimes a Subconscious Self chooses to meet its own needs and exclude the needs of other Selves.

A normal person has multiple Selves that support the Outer Self in maintaining order.

A person can be described as *fragmented*, when her/his Outer Self and Basic Selves are acting in isolation, competition, or conflict, or as *integrated*, when her Outer Self and Basic Selves are communicative, cooperative, and working for the highest good of the entire personality. A person diagnosed as having "multiple personality disorder" has an unusual condition involving dissociated, fragmented Subconscious Selves and a weakened Outer Self that has difficulty maintaining order.

Our research shows that a normal person has multiple Selves that support the Outer Self in *maintaining* order. Multiple personality disorder is forcing the field of psychiatry to reconsider fundamental definitions of personality structure and normality.[12] Some of the techniques of Personal Self Integration are now being used experimentally in psychiatric practice to bring harmony of purpose to competing Selves.

Personal growth occurs when we achieve greater integration of Selves.

Personal growth occurs when we achieve greater *integration* of Selves, expressing benefits that come with integration – love, joy, creativity, competence, etc. Other benefits include improved physical and emotional health, expanded sensitivity to psychic and spiritual dimensions, better memory, and a more coherent and creative life. Through personal growth using Personal Self Integration, we achieve our human potential in expressing the wholeness and oneness of our being.

Integration of the facets of personality expands our understanding of consciousness. Most of the time we limit our identity to that of a "physical body operated by a mind." By expanding this concept to include Subconscious Selves and High Self, we can consider the possibility of a greater, more cohesive organization of our psyche.

When we explore the potential of *intelligent* resources within our Selves, we find that most of this intelligence lies beyond the normal boundaries of our conscious mind, and that access to it requires its *willingness* to be accessed. In addition to our conscious intent, we may need subconscious permission for effective access because the subconscious mind acts as a guardian of inner intelligence. How can we gain access to our inner resources?

Time-honored methods of accessing the inner resources of the subconscious and superconscious levels of mind include prayer, meditation, dream work, trance induction, states of reverie, hypnosis, use of psychoactive drugs, controlled breathing, guided imagery, spontaneous acting out, and various methods for seeking visionary experiences. Such methods become difficult to use when they involve long periods of time, extensive discipline, intensive effort, complicated skills, or someone else's qualified guidance.

Personal Self Integration methods require small to moderate amounts of time, discipline, and effort to accomplish significant results. Most of the Personal Self Integration skills consist mainly of skills we have already developed in *interpersonal* relationships with family and friends. Only a brief period of training is needed to develop inner dialogue skills, and then a person can help herself in significant ways. The first step may involve an actual introduction to Basic Selves.

BASIC SELF DIALOGUE

This "introduction to our subconscious mind" occurs in one or more interviews conducted by an interviewer trained in Personal Self Integration. Once you have been introduced, you can develop the ability to have your own creative and revealing dialogues with your Basic Selves.

The interviewer first asks you to ask your High Self, "Which of my Basic Selves should talk first, male or female?" Your High Self knows best which Basic Self should speak first, especially in cases when Basic Selves have been alienated from each other, fearful of each other, or in competition for your attention. You receive the answer from *your* inner guidance in the form which works best for you – an inner voice, visual symbols, physical sensations, or a sense of knowing.

You respect the Basic Self by accepting the name that he/she has chosen.

The interviewer then asks you to inquire mentally of that Basic Self, "What name do you wish to be called?" You *receive* a name selected by that Basic Self. You respect the Basic Self by accepting the name that he/she has chosen, even if you do not like that name. The names that Basic Selves select are usually symbolic, so you can gain greater understanding of the qualities and purposes of each Basic Self by exploring the meanings and connotations of the names they select.

The interviewer interviews that Basic Self by asking you to allow the Basic Self to answer a set of questions by using your voice. At all times you are fully conscious and in control, yet cooperating with this Self requires you to allow it expression through your voice. You listen to your Basic Self answer the interviewer's questions, letting the words come from another part of your being than if *you*, the Outer Self, were answering. At times you will hear in amazement your Basic Self express viewpoints quite different from yours.

No hypnotic trance state is induced. The Personal Self Integration method promotes expansion of the Outer Self's capability to communicate with deeper levels of mind. You learn that you *can* access intelligence and feelings that normally lie beyond your grasp. You learn to *listen* to this inner intelligence as well as talk with it. In being receptive, you build a beautiful sense of inner trust and companionship that comes with profound internal dialogue.

In being receptive, you build a beautiful sense of inner trust and companionship that comes with profound internal dialogue.

The interview normally continues until you gain information from two Basic Selves representing the masculine and feminine aspects of your subconscious mind. This information includes the perspectives, emotions, thoughts, and aspirations of each Basic Self. These may differ greatly from those of the Outer Self. When the Outer Self respects their views, Basic Selves are more inclined to honor the requests of the Outer Self. Such cooperation gives the Outer Self access to subconscious capabilities.

Inner Self Communication Factors

Meeting an Inner Self is like meeting another person. While you recognize another person as having a separate physical body, you need to use your creative imagination in meeting an Inner Self, which means being open and receptive in perceiving that Self's qualities. Each inner Self has its own distinctive energetic presence. Just as a child learns to sense the distinct energetic presence of its mother and father, so you the Outer Self learn to do the same with your inner Selves.

By using a guided imagery method to facilitate meeting an Inner Self, an Outer Self gains images and impressions with eyes closed. Closing our eyes helps us focus our attention inward and avoid external distractions.

When we are fearful, we tend to keep our eyes open to be alert for threats and stabilize our awareness of the external environment. This fear-based reflex needs to be recognized at the outset of the process so that the interviewer can utilize exercises for reducing fear and optimizing a client's readiness for meeting an inner Self.

When our eyes are open, we focus our awareness on certain perceptive patterns that we have adopted from infancy onward. Focusing our awareness inward requires closing our eyes and opening to internal impressions. In this way, we create new perceptive patterns that give us greater freedom of perception that benefits our life experience in many ways.

Preparation for Guided Imagery

Our practice of meditation and contemplation serves this purpose, facilitating new perceptive discoveries in the realm of consciousness. With eyes closed, we shift our brain and nervous system patterns of perception and reaction, allowing a greater scope of internal perception and more detailed awareness of our states of consciousness. For most persons, it is necessary to shift from fear reactions like, "I can't see!", to peaceful acceptance of whatever consciousness presents.

Research in the field of psychology demonstrates the value of meditation and mindfulness training as methods for stress reduction. And learning to be aware of one's pattern of breathing is also important for achieving stress reduction and readiness for exploring internal states of consciousness.

An effective strategy for preparing a person to meet an Inner Self involves helping her/him to recognize their internal signs of stress in *physical signals*. An interviewer provides a safe, comfortable, and private environment for a client, asks the client to sit or recline, and asks a series of questions that stimulate the client's awareness of internal stress and begin a slow, deep breathing exercise for stress reduction.

With eyes closed, a client is asked to focus on feeling physical sensations in their entire physical body. The interviewer may ask, "How does your entire body feel?" That question prompts global and inclusive awareness in the client. The interviewer cultivates global awareness in the client as a first step and helps the client feel safe and comfortable in describing physical sensations on a total body level.

A client may notice pleasant sensations that contribute to her/his sense of safety, or a client may identify specific areas of pain and discomfort. The interviewer helps the client describe these "trouble spots" and integrate them into global body awareness so that they do not distract the client's awareness. When the client can proceed without distracting physical sensations, the interviewer may proceed to the guided imagery process.

Guided Imagery Process

A person's level of skill in utilizing guided imagery varies. Some persons experience vivid imagery, and others lack any coherent images. Fear and stress reduce a person's ability to "see" and "feel" and "hear" internal awareness. The preparation process just described aids a client in being more capable of perceiving and sharing internal experiences.

An interviewer can assess a client's ability to identify and describe both global and specific physical sensations with eyes closed during the preparation process. Deeper breathing can also be utilized to release stress before doing guided imagery.

In my practice of PSI training, I establish a High Self to High Self telepathic connection *before* starting the training. In that way, my High Self provides me with useful impressions of a client's Inner Selves and gives me cues for guiding the process.

My High Self quickly learns the life plan of the client and her/his strong and weak points in growth. My High Self sends me appropriate information about the client's Subconscious Selves and how they are likely to support or sabotage the guided imagery procedure. It sends that information to each of my Selves so they can prepare themselves to interact with the client's Selves in helpful ways.

Interference from a Mental Judge Self

Usually, a client's Mental Judge Self is most fearful of the process. It often fears that when the Outer Self befriends a Male or Female Self, it will lose influence over that Self and be more at risk from the "predatory" High Self. It tends to view the High Self as seeking to enslave it, weakening its position in its continual power struggle against the High Self. Ironically, the Mental Judge Self projects its own image and harmful intentions upon the High Self who is a Solar Angel, just the opposite of what the Mental Judge Self projects.

All the High Self seeks is the best spiritual growth of the Subconscious Selves, and it is aware of the Mental Judge Self's fears and primary need for safety. The Mental Judge needs to feel that it is in control so that it can feel safe.

If a client's High Self decides that client will best benefit from proceeding with the guided imagery experience, it will distract the Mental Judge from interfering. The High Self prevents the usual fear reactions of the Mental Judge Self by distracting its attention from the personality to somewhere else in the mental plane. That distraction relieves the Male and Female Selves from having to struggle with the Mental Judge's fears and controlling mental messages.

The guided imagery procedure can proceed with greater ease and spontaneity without having to contend with the Mental Judge Self's fears.

Interference from a Basic Self

In seeking to communicate with a Basic Self, its level of trauma might complicate and interfere with the guided images procedure. For example, a Male Self may be traumatized by past life events to a point where he does not want to communicate with any other Self. All he wants to do is remain isolated in his suffering. He may be stuck in a victim role, endlessly recycling his painful memories and blaming himself for his mistakes. He is so intensely involved in his suffering that he does not want to be bothered.

The same reaction may occur in a Female Self who is stuck in a repetitive grieving process involving the loss of a love relationship or loss of control of that relationship. She prefers remaining in an incomplete process of grief in a victim role to achieving forgiveness and moving on to new love relationships. She struggles to value and love herself and does not want to be bothered.

Such reactions of resistance in Basic Selves create disturbance and can prevent a Self's participation in the guided imagery procedure. Yet the client's High Self wishes to encourage a troubled Basic Self's participation. It may prepare the Basic Self to see value in communicating with the Outer

Self during days before the event. It may provide a Loving energetic boost for that Self to lift it temporarily out of its depressed state.

In my practice, my High Self cues me into a client's subconscious reactions so that I can focus communication on meeting immediate needs and then proceed with guided imagery. I and my Inner Selves radiate goodwill, empathy, caring and Love to those Selves of the client, creating an uplift of spirits and motivation to explore their inner relationships.

Interference from an Astral Judge Self

On occasion, I have found that a client's Astral Judge Self has unresolved needs that can interfere with the guided imagery procedure. An Astral Judge Self is less likely to interfere than is the Mental Judge Self. An Astral Judge Self focuses entirely on *feelings*, where a Mental Judge Self focuses on thoughts and power dynamics. An Astral Judge is more like a child experiencing life with a limited understanding. It is very curious about relationships, feels at home in a group or a crowd, and depends on being with other Selves when its safety is threatened. It loves group dancing and musical pageants where it joins with others in a common purpose of celebration.

However, an Astral Judge Self may act like a child who demands attention and caring by preventing or interrupting a guided imagery procedure. In my practice, I'm alerted to that possibility by my High Self, so I ask my Astral Judge Self to communicate with a client's Astral Judge and join in some communal celebration on their level of consciousness.

An interviewer who has not developed that capability may have to deal first with satisfying an Astral Judge Self's needs to gain its cooperation for proceeding with the guided imagery procedure.

Interference from a Body Self

On rare occasions, I have had a client's Body Self interfere with the guided imagery. A Body Self lives in the etheric body that acts as an energetic template for the physical body. It can exacerbate physical symptoms to signal to the Outer Self an urgent need. A Body Self's concern lies in promoting better health in the etheric and physical bodies.

A client with health problems might neglect self-care, placing their Body Self in a stressed position. Their Body Self can sense imbalances and crises occurring in the etheric body that can harm the physical body.

In my experience, a client may suddenly find that a symptom suddenly flares into greater intensity. A small pain might quickly intensify. A shallow breath might become a choking sensation. The physical signal is strong enough to gain the attention of the client's Outer Self and interfere with the guided imagery procedure.

In my practice, the client's High Self will alert me to the Body Self's need when its physical signal appears, and I ask the Body Self to describe what healing is needed, then ask the client's High Self to provide that healing in cooperation with the Body Self. The physical signal diminishes within three to five minutes in using that approach.

An interviewer may use this strategy with similar results, then proceed with the guided imagery procedure.

Guided Imagery Scenarios

Over the years, I have been guided by my High Self to use two scenarios of guided imagery to introduce a client to a Basic Self. I've used the first scenario of "Follow the Path" most of the time in working one-on-one with a client.

In a class situation, I've been guided to use the "Theater" scenario that takes less time, and the other participants learn much from those who share their experience first. And those who share first gain much from those who share later.

On a few occasions when a Mental Judge Self attempts to block the process, I've been guided to use *direct conversation* with a Basic Self to override the interference. Instead of relying on guided imagery that the client's Mental Judge Self disrupts, I speak directly to the Basic Self we wish to meet and ask it to speak to me using the client's voice.

An interviewer is welcome to use these procedures and innovate with High Self guidance to create other procedures that may prove effective.

"Follow the Path" Guided Imagery Procedure

The "Follow the Path" procedure was spontaneously presented to me by my High Self as a thoughtful way of eliciting considerable information about the Basic Self being introduced to the client's Outer Self.

I present here the general structure of the procedure with relevant considerations for interpreting the emerging imagery at key places in the journey of discovery.

Picture Yourself on a Path

Having first guided a client into feeling comfortable with eyes closed, feeling their physical sensations and becoming comfortable with them, experiencing the benefit of deeper, freer breathing, I ask them, **"Picture yourself on a path that leads to the home of your Male/Female Self** (whichever applies)." I send goodwill and supportive energy to the client and observe their state of receptivity with my High Self's help.

Next, I ask the client, **"Please describe your path."** That request prompts the client to speak out loud in describing their internal path. By speaking out loud, a client establishes a link not only with me, but also assists their Outer Self in feeling safe and comfortable in that new situation.

A client may give a brief or lengthy description in describing their path. If their description is brief, I ask, **"Please describe how your path proceeds in the environment."** This request gives a client opportunity to expand their internal awareness and describe their path in more detail and include the environment through which their path moves.

If a client has difficulty following their path, I ask them to **"Please deepen your breathing."** As their stress level declines with deeper breathing, I ask, **"Is your path easy or difficult to follow?"**

If a client replies, "Difficult," I ask, **"What makes it difficult?"** Some clients say, "It's dark, and the path keeps twisting and going up and down."

I interpret these details and keep them to myself at that point. When a client's imagery presents *darkness* that makes it difficult to follow their path, it often suggests a lack of awareness of their personality's subconscious level of consciousness. This reaction often suggests that the client has experienced nightmares and traumatic experiences beginning in childhood, and they have deep-seated fears that distract the Outer Self from probing their subconscious memories. They literally have shined too little "light of awareness" into their subconscious mind to perceive a path of healing those traumas.

A similar experience of darkness occurs when a client says that their path must go through dark areas of a dense forest or a tunnel in a mountain. Those conditions offer evidence that the Outer Self has experienced some breakthroughs in opening some awareness of their subconscious dynamics.

The darkness and density of the materials that obstruct progress on the path also express valuable insights. For example, if the darkness in their imagery makes the Outer Self feel that it's impossible to illuminate the path, that condition offers evidence that the Outer Self has *no* awareness of what blocks its perception. In that case, an Outer Self feels helpless and defeated by some unknown interference.

When a client finds that its path if darkened by a dense forest or jungle, that symbolism suggests conflict with *subconscious compulsions*. A forest and a jungle are composed of *wood*, and subconsciously that symbol translates "wood" into "would," "should," "have to," and "ought to," words that express compulsion. These obstacles on the path reveal reactions of "right" and "wrong" on ethical levels of behavior, and reactions of "good" and "evil" behavior on a religious or theological level. An attentive interviewer will gain valuable insights from such observations.

The greater or lesser *density* of obstacles on the path suggest the fundamental attitude of the client in dealing with personal challenges. A huge boulder or an avalanche that blocks progress on the path often suggests a subconscious attitude of *defeat* that no matter how much effort is expended or how much help is supplied, any progress on the path is *impossible*.

This attitude of defeat reveals a situation where one or more Subconscious Selves have reacted to Lessons of Power presented by the High Self by *refusing* to use their power in achieving progress on the path. A Mental Judge Self can refuse the use of power to itself and one or both Basic Selves when it is frustrated with itself. It can manipulate the awareness and concepts of either or both Basic Selves to create *mutual refusal* to use power.

When I confront an attitude of defeat and it appears that progress on the path is blocked, I bring High Self power into the imagery to overcome the attitude of defeat. I first acknowledge the attitude and attribute it to intense fears expressed by one or more Subconscious Selves.

"I find that this obstacle on the path is only an attitude based on fears held by your Subconscious Selves. Since it's only fear that restrains your progress on the path, I now call on the power of your High Self and my High Self to remove this resistance so that you can continue your path. Please breathe more deeply."

Each time that this request is made, the client can proceed on the path through the intervention of the High Selves.

Other obstacles on the path may appear, including *antagonists* who can be overcome with some understanding of what inner conflicts they represent and intervention by the High Self. On rare occasions, an Outer Self will be *unable to locate the home* of the Basic Self they wish to meet. That situation is due to interference by a Mental Judge Self who wishes to avoid its own exposure and identification by the Outer Self.

When a client has *no difficulty* in following the path to the home of Basic Self, an interviewer is assured of *cooperation* in the process instead of resistance. I ask, **"Now see in the distance the home of your Male/Female Basic Self. Notice its appearance."**

Arrival at the Self's Home

This distant view of the Basic Self's home promotes personal safety when the Outer Self glimpses the home. It can gain initial impressions about that Basic Self's way of living without having the pressure of directly meeting that Self.

The Outer Self's distant view of the Basic Self's home reveals significant information about that Self's values and acceptance of the world in which it resides. For example, the Outer Self may notice that the home is in plain view or hidden. Being in plain view suggests that Self's openness for social and personal relationships. Conversely, a home hidden from others implies a need for privacy or social isolation. These distant observations provide significant insights about the Basic Self before meeting it.

After noting these observations, I ask, **"Now see yourself near the**

front door of your Self's home. Breathe, and notice how you feel being there."

This arrival at the Basic Self's home offers further impressions about that Self, as well as noticing the Outer Self's reactions to being there. The Outer Self may feel completely at ease, which often indicates familiarity with that Basic Self. Or the Outer Self may feel uncomfortable, ill at ease, and even fearful of being near that Basic Self.

For example, the Outer Self may notice that the home appears dilapidated and needs much repair, suggesting that the Basic Self does not wish to maintain acceptable social appearances, or wishes to discourage visitors. The appearance of the home reflects a combination of Basic Self intentions and Outer Self reactions. The Outer Self may have formed prejudiced views of the Basic Self and discovers such views in this stage of the process.

If the Outer Self feels ready to meet that Basic Self, I ask it, **"In your own words, please express your purpose for coming here to meet this Basic Self. Please say them out loud."** This request gives the Outer Self an opportunity to express its desire to not only meet the Basic Self, but also to form a friendship for mutual benefit.

When the Outer Self completes its message, I ask, **"How do you feel in having shared that with your Basic Self?"** This request allows the Outer Self opportunity to express its positive or negative reactions about its statement of purpose with concerns about the Basic Self's reaction to what was shared.

Meeting a Basic Self

Now ask this Self, **"Please come to greet me."** And here the Outer Self has an opportunity to see an image of the Basic Self. If the Outer Self has confidence and desires to meet the Basic Self, an image quickly forms of the Basic Self opening the front door of its home and emerging with an attitude of welcoming. This positive reception occurs when both Outer Self and Basic Self express their desires to meet and befriend each other.

If either Self is caught in fear, this step in the guided imagery process may result in the following experiences:

- The Basic Self does *not* present an image because it holds fears about how the Outer Self might react to it. This situation often occurs when the Basic Self has adopted a negative self-image associated with guilt, shame, and unworthiness.
- The Outer Self feels fear of meeting the Basic Self due to the Outer Self holding a negative self-image associated with guilt, shame, and unworthiness.
- A physical circumstance distracts the Outer Self, such as telephone ringing, a sudden pain in their body, or a need to urinate.

When the guided imagery process stalls at this crucial point, it might be necessary to shift from imagery to a discussion with the client's eyes open in reviewing what happened and identifying emotional reactions of the Outer Self and Basic Self. The goal consists of creating a better understanding of what happened and reducing the fears experienced by Outer Self and Basic Self. The guided imagery process can be continued at a later date, and in the interim the Outer Self may be willing to send goodwill and even love to the Basic Self. It's important to encourage a deliberate shift from fear-based reactions to expressions of compassion on the part of both Selves.

Various scenarios can take place in the guided imagery process that express difficulty in achieving this meeting of Selves:

- **When an Outer Self says out loud, "Please come to greet me," the Basic Self stays hidden behind the front door.** In that case, the Basic Self does not yet feel ready to face the Outer Self, so it consents to talk but not present itself. The Outer Self can accept the opportunity to talk with the Basic Self by expressing its positive intentions and asking the Basic Self some questions that might relieve the Basic Self's concerns, such as "I am here to be your friend, so how can I help you?" and "I realize that I have ignored you for a long time, so what can I do that will help you talk with me?"
- **When a Basic Self says, "Go away! Don't bother me."** In that situation, it's important to have the Outer Self press the Basic Self for an explanation of its refusal to meet the Outer Self. The Outer

Self may ask the Basic Self, "I have a right to know what motivates you to reject meeting me. What benefit do you gain from staying separate from me?" That direct question encourages the Basic Self to identify its motivation, which is typically based on fear of discovery that it has burdened itself with negative self-judgments.

- **When a Basic Self presents a cartoon image of itself.** In that case, the Basic Self shows that it is not ready to fully reveal itself. The image it offers often has symbolic value. For example, a Female Self might present the image of Snow White and/or the Wicked Queen as a way of suggesting that she is striving to be morally pure, yet sometimes expresses selfish or evil intentions. A Male Self might offer an image of a mighty warrior, an image of Popeye the Sailor, or a hurt abused child.

- **When a Basic Self presents itself as a monster.** In rare cases, the Basic Self presents its image as a monster intended to frighten and repel the Outer Self. This reaction is often associated with childhood traumas.

These varied responses of the Basic Self are based on its fears of being known as "less than" how it wishes to be known. The Outer Self is wise to recognize that the Basic Self has lived hundreds of physical lifetimes and made numerous mistakes that it has come to regret. It might feel more like a burden than a resource for the Outer Self. A Male Self may feel ashamed of its abuses of power over others as the High Self directed him in learning the Lessons of Power. A Female Self learning the Lessons of Love might regret her selfish manipulation of others to keep her personal love secure.

Receiving the Name of a Basic Self

Having seen the image presented by the Basic Self, the Outer Self asks, "What name do you wish to be called?" This important step of identification may result in the following scenarios:

- **A Basic Self presents a single name** that the Outer Self needs to accept and use to show respect for the Basic Self. In some cases, the Outer Self may easily accept the name and be interested in what the name implies about the Basic Self. For example, the name "Mary" might have a special meaning if the Outer Self identifies it with Mary, the mother of Jesus. In other cases, the name "George" represents a more casual friendship that is easy to cultivate.

- **A Basic Self offers more than one alternative names**, causing confusion in the Outer Self. The Outer Self needs to ask the Basic Self to *select one of those names* to make it easy for the Outer Self to remember. The Outer Self may say, "Please select only one name to make it easy for me to communicate with you. It's important for the Outer Self to recognize that the Basic Self has used many names in many lifetimes. Normally, Basic Selves communicate with telepathy and do not rely on physical human names.

- **A Basic Self selects a name symbolic of positive potential** with abilities that the Outer Self can recognize, support, and cultivate in that Basic Self. For example, the name "Ruth" may refer to the story of Ruth in *The Bible*, suggesting that the Outer Self may find value in sustaining a challenging marriage. Or the name "Rama" may imply the value of the Outer Self acting decisively in resolving conflicts in a close but troubled relationship.

Touring the Home of a Basic Self

When an Outer Self has received and accepted the name presented by the Basic Self, it needs to gain greater insight into the values and preferences of the Basic Self. A reasonable approach in that tentative relationship involves the Outer Self asking the Basic Self for a tour of its home. The Outer Self asks, **"Would you please give me a tour of your home?"** And the following options might occur:

- **The Basic Self opens the front door and invites the Outer Self in.** In that case, a Basic Self is willing to share more of how she/he lives. The Outer Self is wise to notice the color scheme and décor of the home. Is it well-lit or dark inside? Does the décor express harmony or disharmony? Does the home seem comfortable for visitors or seem to be an unvisited place for a solitary Basic Self? The décor and colors of the home express many value states, such as cheerfulness or depression. Does the home display many books? Do the windows focus on the beauty of nature in the landscape? Is there a closed door that the Basic Self does not wish to open?

- **The Basic Self invites the Outer Self to look through the open front door, but not enter the home.** This behavior shows the Outer Self that the Basic Self is not yet willing to reveal much more about itself and its values. In that case, the Outer Self needs to recognize that it needs to build greater trust in that relationship. When the Basic Self becomes more trusting of the intentions of the Outer Self, it will be willing to invite the Outer Self into its home.

- **The Basic Self refuses to let the Outer Self enter the home.** This situation shows that the Basic Self does not yet feel secure enough to let the Outer Self tour its home. Its reaction is triggered by fear that might be based on its experience of personal betrayal by others in prior lifetimes. In that case, the Outer Self is wise to take extra steps in relating with the Basic Self to demonstrate positive intentions that promote the development of trust within the Basic Self. Periodically, the Outer Self can ask the Basic Self if it feels ready to give the Outer Self a tour of its home.

Asking Questions of a Basic Self

When a Basic Self seems open to share its values, an Outer Self can ask it strategic questions, relationship questions, and experiential questions that refer to specific experiences of the Outer Self. It's important to make notes of the Basic Self's answers.

The list of **general strategic questions** that I commonly present to the Outer Self to ask the Basic Self as it tours the home includes the following:

- What do you most love and enjoy?
- What do you fear and seek to avoid?
- What are your major interests?
- What are your major goals?
- Where do you need some help?
- How can I, the Outer Self, provide that help for you?

These questions provide a useful perspective of how the Basic Self lives, what it values, and what it seeks.

They may be followed later by **specific relationship questions**:

- How do you relate to the other Basic Self (Male or Female)?
- What is your view of her/him?
- What would you like to improve in that relationship?
- How can you begin discussing that improvement with her/him?
- Do you need some help from me and the High Self in starting that discussion?
- When will you be ready to start that discussion?
- Are you willing to receive prayers of support?

These specific relationship questions can refer to any of the Selves of the personality, not only the other Basic Self, if that seems appropriate.

Experiential questions can often be revealing about the Basic Self being introduced. When an Outer Self has had some experiences that might relate to the Basic Self, it may be helpful to ask it if it was involved in producing those experiences. For example, the Outer Self may have searched for guidance in opening an inspirational book to a passage that offers guidance. Or the Outer Self may have been shopping and found her/his car dented by another car. Or the Outer Self may have had a scary or uplifting dream within days before the PSI session.

The Outer Self may ask the Basic Self the following questions:

- Were you involved in giving me the experience of _____?
- What did you seek to communicate to me?
- Do you feel that I'm not listening to you?
- What can I do to be more aware of your messages?
- If you weren't involved, which other Self was involved?

As the Outer Self learns more about the needs of Subconscious Selves, she/he becomes motivated to recognize their inner telepathic messages. That positive response makes it less likely that a Subconscious Self will have to resort to manifesting external experiences that invite the Outer Self to listen to its messages.

This guided imagery process of introducing a Basic Self also may be used with other Subconscious Selves. It offers a series of gradual steps for the Outer Self to follow in opening communication with a given Self. If a client does not achieve a definite meeting with a Subconscious Self the first time, she/he may be encouraged to try the process until it works.

"Theater" Guided Imagery Procedure

The "theater" procedure was spontaneously presented to me by my High Self as a quicker way of eliciting helpful information about more than one Basic Self in a class setting. I share an information sheet about the seven Selves identified in the PSI model, spending at least ten minutes to help the participants recognize characteristic behaviors of those Inner Selves. I announce that "With our time limits, we will limit meeting just two or three of the seven. In a class of more than twenty persons at an international conference, I use this "theater" format:

- I ask my High Self to connect with the High Selves of all the participants.
- I ask the participants to align their chairs in a circle, so that I am in the center of the circle.
- I explain the process: "First, we'll briefly meet our Inner Selves, learn their names, see their images, and feel how they react to us. You may wish to make some notes about each Self, and I'll give you a couple of minutes to do that. When we have met these Selves, we will share what we have learned. We will meet our Female Self, Male Self, and Mental Judge Self in sequence.
- I guide the group by having them close their eyes, take five deeper breaths, and feel how their physical body feels.
- I observe their energy fields to identify any participants who might have difficulty with the process.
- I ask the group to use their imagination in the guided imagery process and rely on their feeling sensitivity to gain information about their Inner Selves if it's difficult for them to visualize.
- I ask the group to be in the front rows of a theater where the stage curtain is closed.

- I ask them how they feel being there.
- As the theater announcer, I ask them to be aware that when I open the curtain on the stage, they will meet their Female Self.
- I count to three out loud and announce, "As the curtain opens, please welcome your Female Self!"
- I say, "In your mind, please tell her that you wish to be her friend and really want to get to know her. Notice how she responds, and notice her appearance."
- I say, "Ask her how she feels about meeting and talking with you."
- I say, "Ask her what name she wishes to be called."
- I say, "What does she wish to tell you?"
- I say, "Please respond to her from your heart."
- I say, "Ask her if she is willing to talk with you about her concerns."
- I say, "Now thank her for talking with you."
- I say, "Now slowly open your eyes and write your notes about her."

After a few minutes of note-writing, I repeat the process in meeting their Male Self. Then we proceed with the Mental Judge Self and the High Self. Then I ask participants to share their experiences with the Female Self first, appreciating the similarities and differences. Each group sharing needs to be at least ten minutes in duration.

We continue sharing about the other Selves, and I suggest some further communication steps that participants might use to continue and deepen their relationship with their Selves. Some participants may wish to contact me to have further training in PSI.

The Theater format offers a brief way of engaging persons with some of their Inner Selves and demonstrating to them how they can further develop the quality of communication with them.

"Direct Communication" Procedure

The "Direct Communication" procedure was spontaneously presented to me by my High Self in a situation when a client's Mental Judge Self attempted to block or distort the guided imagery procedure, yet the client's High Self required that I override this attempt to control the communication.

In this case, as a client's Mental Judge Self or other Subconscious Self attempted to block the guided imagery introduction, the client's High Self asked me to open direct communication with the desired Basic Self and maintain that focus, as their High Self quieted and diverted the interfering Self's attention elsewhere.

In the Direct Communication situation, I ask the desired Self to talk with me directly in using the client's voice. I ask my High Self to guide the process and even form key questions of the client's desired Self, which is often a Male Self or a Female Self.

We focus on how that Self feels about another Self's interference, and what assistance the desired Self needs in that moment and on an ongoing basis. We confirm that Self's request with the client's High Self and follow through immediately if its need is immediate.

For example, a Male Self attempts to free himself from a habit of negatively judging himself as prompted by the Mental Judge Self. The Mental Judge Self fears that it is losing control of the Male Self, so it blocks the guided imagery process and undermines contact with the Male Self. The High Self of the client then intervenes to divert the Mental Judge Self and its attempt at sabotage, making it possible for me to ask the Male Self to talk about his needs. I ask questions and receive direct responses from the Male Self, speaking with the client's voice.

BASIC SELF CHARACTERISTICS

Personal Self Integration views Basic Selves as a subject for ongoing research that gives a person the opportunity to make his or her own discoveries about Basic Selves. In this way, the base of personal research experience is broadened sufficiently to reveal the influence of personal and cultural biases that might distort perceptions of Basic Selves. Personal Self Integration represents an expansion of the spiritual research of Drs. Guthrie and Karish.

Vehicles of Spiritual Growth

The 30 years of spiritual research by Guthrie and Karish identifies Basic Selves as crucial elements for the spiritual evolution of a personality. Their book, *Pathways to Your Three Selves (1989)*, presents their findings about a system for understanding the mechanisms of spiritual growth. Their findings are summarized here as a starting point for validation and discovery through further research. Their model of Three Selves is related to the spiritual practices of the Kahunas of Hawaii and Polynesia that deal with a Low Self, a Middle Self, and a High Self.

Guthrie and Karish report that when a Soul comes from the cosmos to participate in planet Earth, it links with a High Self that selects Basic Selves to provide an earthly vehicle for the Soul's evolution. In this model, Basic Selves are assigned roles within a plan for spiritual growth known as a *master karmic plan*, devised by the High Self and a Master Teacher. The plan provides Basic Selves with the experience of numerous embodiments (lifetimes) as physical personalities for learning lessons that lead to their ultimate goal of becoming High Selves. Thus Basic Selves are seen as prime *achievers of spiritual growth*.

In this viewpoint, a personality's karmic plan is designed to aid all elements of the human personality and the Soul that gives it life and purpose. The karmic plan provides a series of experiences that enable the Soul to learn and master its lessons. Because the Soul needs to relate to Earth experience through some kind of vehicle, it expresses its qualities and dynamic will primarily through the Basic Selves and secondarily through the Outer Self. This arrangement is like our country sending automated space probes to the moon or other planets, where conditions might be harmful to us. Basic Selves can be seen as "space probes" that enable the Soul to learn through Earth experience and increase its ability to return ultimately as a perfected form to God, the Source of life.

The Basic Selves can be seen as "space probes"
that enable the Soul to learn through Earth
experience and increase its ability to return ultimately
as a perfected form to God, the Source of life.

In this capacity, Basic Selves are assisted by the Outer Self, which begins its evolution with the birth of a new physical body. In comparison, the Outer Self is like a "new-comer" while Basic Selves are like "old-timers." At the death of the physical body, an Outer Self's energies are translated into nonphysical energies that become part of the Basic Selves. The Outer Self is not lost, but reunited with all other Outer Selves sponsored by the ongoing personality. Basic Selves incorporate the memories of all the Outer Selves with which they have been associated. This accumulation of experience makes Basic Selves usually more knowledgeable than Outer Selves.

Basic Selves are described as entering the physical body of a fetus after conception. They influence the physical body through the region located between the top vertebra of the spine and the base of the skull known as the alta major chakra. Their influence operates largely through the brain and nervous system as a web that has connections with the chakras, glands, and organs of the body. They draw much of their energy from the solar plexus area of the abdomen, an area often associated with the function of the subconscious mind. In comparison, the influence of the Soul is described as operating through the thymus or heart chakra, and that of the spirit as through the circulatory system of the body.

Free Will

One important aspect to consider is that a Basic Self has its own free will. It is not a slave to the Outer Self or a computer waiting to be programmed, as many popular books have suggested. A Basic Self represents an extension of the Soul's free will; it functions as a vehicle for Soul in applying free will in Earth experience. The term *will* is defined as the ability to make choices and decisions. It represents the most dynamic and crucial aspect of the Soul since the Soul grows mainly through its choices.

A Basic Self represents an extension of the Soul's free will.

Personal Self Integration recognizes the free will of Basic Selves and trains the Outer Self to communicate and negotiate with its Basic Selves. The Outer Self also derives its free will from Soul, so it may choose to acknowledge greater powers than itself or not. An Outer Self might deny other Selves, higher powers, and its need for growth, yet it ultimately finds itself bound by conditions beyond its power. The same holds true for a Basic Self. Both Outer Self and Basic Self are directed and assisted by a supervising High Self that administers a plan for growth.

Spiritual growth requires learning both knowledge and skills that expand a Self's capacity for accepting and expressing what Soul offers to the evolution of the planet. Each Self of a personality must evolve to express a willingness to cooperate with Soul and become more like Soul in expressing intentions of universal benefit. However, most Selves focus on their own selfish needs and desires early in their evolution. The High Self must guide them into making choices that open them beyond selfishness into altruism.

The *qualities* of Basic Selves are composed of some of the qualities of the cosmos, some dynamic structures and styles of consciousness found within the universe. Soul utilizes these qualities like building blocks of life to create and sustain a personality. We will briefly explore these qualities that characterize the Selves of a personality, extending the current model of psychology into areas of spiritual research.

In Guthrie and Karish's work, Basic Selves are described as having five areas of characteristics that affect their ability to live and relate with each other:

1. Sexual polarities.
2. States of integration.
3. Self-esteem.
4. Relationship stages.
5. Styles of universal consciousness.

These characteristics combine to provide specific identities for Basic Selves who seem like "inner persons" to us, with all the interesting complexities that we might associate with a friend.

Sexual Polarities

Basic Selves are normally masculine or feminine in quality. Usually a person has one masculine and one feminine Basic Self. The qualities of a masculine or *Male* Basic Self include strength, will, and determination. The qualities of a feminine or *Female* Basic Self include love, compassion, emotionality, and sensitivity. Masculinity and femininity are seen as opposite polarities of gender energy that each person expresses in varying degrees and ways. Guthrie and Karish's work suggests that the evolutionary goal of Basic Selves involves their acceptance of the opposite polarity and blending with it until male and female Basic Selves merge into an androgynous state of being. Achieving an energetic state of androgynous being brings the personality into closer rapport with androgynous Soul.

The evolutionary goal of Basic Selves involves their acceptance of the opposite polarity and blending with it.

A male Basic Self expresses masculinity, ranging from macho to gentlemanly qualities depending upon his level of evolution. A crude, "male chauvinist" type of Basic Self has little awareness of the feminine polarity and needs to learn more about it. He needs to learn, through successive lifetimes, how to relate to the *wholeness* of life through relating to his opposite polarity and eventually uniting with it. The same evolutionary pattern holds true for a female Basic Self who approaches the goal from the opposite polarity. The expression of *heterosexuality* (male and female partnership) constitutes most of the evolutionary path of a personality.

As evolution of the sexual polarities continues, Guthrie and Karish report that a male Basic Self must learn how to be responsible in caring for *female* physical and emotional bodies, and a female Basic Self in caring for *male* physical and emotional bodies. For one or more lifetimes, this arrangement creates *homosexuality*, as the Basic Self of one polarity seeks to accept the opposite polarity.

From this viewpoint, a male Basic Self still desires to express as a male, even when he is placed within a female body. The same situation occurs for a female Basic Self who is placed in a male body, when she still desires to express as a female. As a Basic Self accepts the body and energies of the opposite polarity, it adapts and learns how to express those energies with increasing skill. A personality may experience a series of lifetimes in male bodies, then a series in female bodies, followed by a series of lifetimes in which male and female Basic Selves learn how to live together harmoniously.

At the point where male and female Basic Selves fully accept each other and can manifest each other's qualities, they blend in a state of androgynous being that accelerates their spiritual growth. Where their earlier homosexual state often exhibited imbalances, the later androgynous state exemplifies balance and harmony. As unified male and female energies, androgynous Basic Selves evolve into High Selves. At this time the Soul may have completed its course of learning on planet Earth and is free to leave or return for another incarnation with a new team of High Self and Basic Selves in another new personality.

States of Polarity Integration

According to Guthrie and Karish, the spiritual evolution of Basic Selves involves a gradual integration of sexual polarities over many embodiments. They name three states of integrated relationships between male and female Basic Selves:

1. A "single" state, where only one polarity - male or female - is expressed.
2. A "dual on a single stem" state, where male and female polarities are blending.
3. An "androgynous" state, where unification of polarities is taking place.

Each state of integration represents the ability of Basic Selves to function on a higher level of the karmic plan. As Basic Selves progress to successive states, they become capable of demonstrating successively greater degrees of wisdom and competence, culminating in a unified state of androgynous male-female consciousness that qualifies them for achieving High Self status.

Single State

As the male and female Basic Selves begin learning and transforming in the personality's karmic plan, they stand as single or separate Basic Selves, existing side by side like two distinct individuals. Each tends to focus on her/his own needs, building sufficient individuality or strength of selfhood to withstand the tests of the karmic plan. A single Basic Self evolves from *insecure* feelings of doubt, fear, mistrust, etc., to *secure* feelings of confidence, faith, trust, etc. In a gradual process, a single Basic Self develops *self-esteem* based on its own sense of worth and its ability to love and care for itself. A single Basic Self selects a name that the Outer Self can use in reaching out to it in dialogue or prayer.

Figure 4 portrays the transformation of Basic Selves through these three phases of interaction. The arrows in the diagram represent the *sutratma*, the constant flow of Life Force from Soul through the personality that Soul sustains. In the single state, the Female and Male Basic Selves are energized separately from the sutratma. In the dual on a stem state, they begin to share Life Force from Soul. During this stage, either or both Selves might choose a new name that reflects their closer relationship. As they learn to accept, care for, and love each other, they blend their feminine and masculine qualities and eventually achieve an androgynous state of integrated gender qualities like Soul qualities. In the process, the unified Self selects a new name portraying its unified expression. Thus Soul achieves a powerful unification of the polarized energies of Earth's lower planes of life, aiding the evolution of the planetary being of Earth, which is one of Soul's purposes.

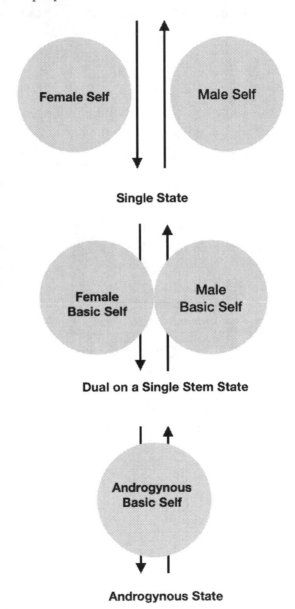

Figure 4. Basic Self States of Integration

During their integrative journey, Basic Selves evolve not only in their relationship with each other, but also in their individual states of *selfhood*. In the early lifetimes of their journey, they develop *internal* qualities that express their individuality. A crucial quality that they need to cultivate is Self-esteem. Psychological studies recognize the value of a person attaining positive self-esteem with the assumption that a person has only one Self. Guthrie and Karish's research shows that assumption is false.

The process of integration requires that each Basic Self clear limiting beliefs and negative judgments that spark conflict within each Self and their relationship. Each Self must develop a deep sense of safety and security within itself, and that platform of Self-esteem facilitates the establishment of trust and security in their relationship. In addition, a Basic Self's detoxification of limiting beliefs and negative judgments opens the Self for deeper connection and communication with the High Self with all the benefits that brings.

Limiting Beliefs

Low Self-esteem is based on a Self's limiting beliefs that are learned in a state of illusion in the early lifetimes of a personality. Life circumstances for a personality and its Selves are organized by the High Self to facilitate spiritual growth. A Self has opportunities to try out different reactions to its experiences. In the mix of daily life, the Outer Self or a Subconscious Self makes unwise choices and harmful decisions that might become habitual reactions that persist over many lifetimes. These illusion-generated reactions and behaviors persist until a Self exerts creative choices to extinguish those intentions and find better choices.

Negative Judgments

A Basic Self also develops learned reactions that produce negative judgments about itself and others. Negative judgments include blaming, shaming, condemning, etc. When a Self feels fearful and insecure, it often empowers itself by making negative judgments. Typically, a Self blames someone or something else. This behavior produces a feeling of empowerment, as opposed to feeling disappointment and discouragement. However, negative judgments rebound on a Self because they contribute to its limiting beliefs, stereotypes, and aggressive behavior. Gradually a Self learns to free itself from resorting to negative judgments and opens perception to higher states of consciousness that foster compassion and love.

Dual on a Single Stem State

When the High Self and Master Teacher decide that the single male and female Basic Selves are ready to be joined on a single stem, they are given a trial period to determine how well they relate to each other and handle their responsibilities. Sometimes they fail the test and are once again separated for one or more embodiments until they re-qualify for integration. Several attempts may occur before this state of integration is achieved.

The state of being "dual on a single stem" can be described as the progressive joining of the two independent Basic Selves in a state of increasing *interdependence*. The High Self creates conditions which promote their joining, such as stimulating them to adopt similar goals and ideals which draw them together. As two persons who share the same or similar goals, learn how to help each other, so do Basic Selves.

The term "on a single stem," also implies a shared source of life or power that animates the Basic Selves with a greater sense of unity than when they were single and independent. Like two flowers on a stem, the Basic Selves express two aspects of an underlying vitality or life force which unifies their efforts.

---

*Like two flowers on a stem, the Basic Selves
express two aspects of an underlying vitality
or life force which unifies their efforts.*

During the state of being "dual on a single stem," Basic Selves work together with greater harmony than when they were single. Their relationship involves increasing awareness and acceptance of the other, much as partnership develops between two people. Their differences are revealed as the karmic plan progresses, enabling them to resolve their difficulties with each other. Consequently, their motivation and ability to be good partners gradually increases over a period of one or more lifetimes.

Androgynous State

The High Self determines if the Basic Selves are ready to become androgynous. This decision is based on how well Basic Selves have matured within the "dual on a single stem" state. When they enter the androgynous state, Basic Selves blend their mental and astral bodies in a process of uniting masculine and feminine polarities.

In their mental bodies, they develop compatible beliefs, perceptions, and reactions through a process of expressing similar *intentions*. The more they both express intentions of universal benefit expressed by Soul, the more compatible they become. Their mental bodies complement each other in creative ways. For example, a Female Self may find that she can function more effectively as an intuitive channel gaining relevant information from the High Self and Soul, while the Male Self works effectively in implementing that information in the actions of the personality by collaborating with the Outer Self.

Their astral bodies evolve as they each experience positive and negative experiences that give them habitual expressions of desires, emotions, attitudes, and expectations. They each encounter lessons of power and love. Through karmic return, they learn the value of releasing traumatic reactions, releasing residual emotions and attitudes from past lives, and clearing most of their fears. This process of astral cleansing leads to a simplified set of astral dynamics that no longer distract from learning lessons and taking actions based on Soul intentions of universal benefit.

They have each demonstrated their ability to function as either male or female if the need should arise, with the wisdom to handle virtually all human situations and relationships. Their transition into a state of androgyny occurs near the end of their sequence of lifetimes as they become more like the High Self.

When they enter the androgynous state,
Basic Selves blend their mental and astral bodies in a process of uniting
masculine and feminine polarities.

If Basic Selves fail to complete the state of androgyny, due to some unresolved misunderstanding, misinterpretation, or other infraction of the karmic plan, they may be returned by the High Self to the state of single Basic Selves and required once again to climb the ladder of evolution.

When Basic Selves complete their lessons of androgynous being, they "graduate" to become a High Self who has the demonstrated the mastery needed to assist other Basic Selves in their evolution. With the achievement of full androgyny, Basic Selves fulfill the condition of resolved polarity that frees the Soul from Earth for further evolution.

Self-Esteem

In the practice of Personal Self Integration, a therapist needs to assess the levels of wellbeing of both Basic Selves early in the process. A state of wellbeing consists of a Self doing more than surviving. It involves capacity for Self-empowerment, enjoyment, and Self realization through creative expression of Soul intentions.

If both Basic Selves feel *insecure*, the Outer Self probably needs assistance in developing Self-esteem in at least one Basic Self. If one Basic Self has a moderate or high level of Self-esteem, the Outer Self can ask it to assist in developing Self-esteem in the other Basic Self. A Basic Self possessing high Self-esteem is more aware, caring, and interested in helping other Selves, while a Basic Self with low Self-esteem is less aware, less caring, and less interested in the welfare of others.

Self-esteem is accomplished one Self at a time,
accumulating within the personality.

In assessing the state of wellbeing of Basic Selves, it is important to identify their levels of Self-esteem at the outset. Conventional psychology addresses Self-esteem only on a total personality level. Inner Selves are usually not recognized. Personal Self Integration evaluates levels of Self-esteem for all Inner Selves, especially the Basic Selves.

Self-esteem represents a Self's overall sense of self-worth or personal value. How well does a Self accept and appreciate itself? This assessment involves a variety of beliefs held by a Self regarding its appearance, role, emotions, and behaviors within a social context.

Self-esteem can be low, moderate, or high. Low Self-esteem represents a state where a Self's needs are *not* being met. Moderate Self-esteem occurs when most of a Self's needs are being met. And high Self-esteem results when virtually all a Self's needs are met.

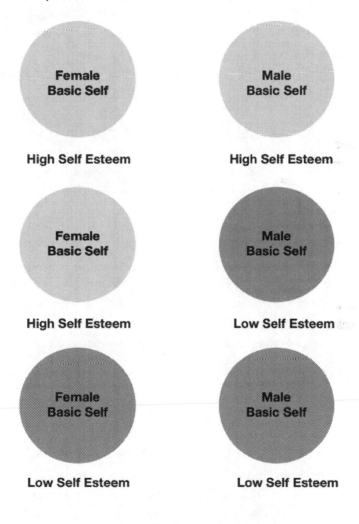

Figure 5. Self Esteem of Basic Selves

Figure 5. Self Esteem of Basic Selves

Maslow's Hierarchy of Needs applies to Basic Selves as well as to the personality as a whole. A Basic Self, having its fundamental needs met, develops Self-esteem, while a Basic Self with unmet fundamental needs does not. An Outer Self can perform a vital task in seeking a Basic Self's perceptions of how well its needs are being met. If a Basic Self feels like it might not survive, is unsafe, does not belong, is unloved or incompetent, an Outer Self can assist it in meeting those fundamental needs. Since Self-esteem is based upon a Self's perception of its *quality of being*, a Basic Self can be assisted by reviewing its perceptions of how its fundamental needs are being met. A Basic Self may have accurate or inaccurate perceptions of its value that the Outer Self can question and validate through repeated observations over time.

Single Basic Selves are likely to have lower Self-esteem
than Basic Selves who have joined on a single stem.

Single Basic Selves are likely to have lower Self-esteem than Basic Selves who have joined on a single stem. Single Basic Selves are also likely to be less competent in performing their responsibilities than those who have joined on a single stem. Having higher Self-esteem aids a Basic Self in achieving competence in handling its responsibilities, and its development of competence aids its development of higher Self-esteem. Thus single Basic Selves develop elementary levels of Self-esteem *and* competence that prepare them for higher states of integration.

Relationship Stages

The High Self assigns specific responsibilities to each Basic Self with the intention of building individual capability. As a single Basic Self meets the challenges of these responsibilities, he/she gains *performance abilities*, such as the ability to keep the physical body healthy or the emotions in balance. A single Basic Self might struggle with an assigned responsibility, sometimes feeling incompetent, yet eventually she/he gains *competence* in handling responsibilities.

---

*They progress through relationship stages of alienation,
co-existence, conflict, competition, and cooperation.*

As male and female single Basic Selves develop Self-esteem and competence, they progress through *relationship stages* of alienation, co-existence, conflict, competition, and cooperation. (See Fig. 6) These subconscious interactions exert a powerful influence on the Outer Self who struggles to be a better person. An important lesson to learn here involves answering the question: *Who* needs to do the learning?

An Outer Self is created as a new entity when a personality that has lived many lifetimes enters a baby body. The new Outer Self has *not* learned the skills of living, so it relies mainly on subconscious impulses and reactions. Conventional psychology views those subconscious or unconscious impulses and reactions as coming from the physical body and its genetic structure. This viewpoint represents a physical-only mechanistic bias that denies a spiritual dimension of being human. Yet overwhelming, rigorous scientific data have verified these psychic abilities that do not fit the narrow mechanistic model. For example, demonstrations of precognition, psychokinesis, and remote viewing are not explainable in that model.

Personal Self Integration operates within a more expansive model of understanding that recognizes the role of subconscious and superconscious aspects of a personality. It utilizes the intelligence of our internal resources. Instead of wondering about the needs of an Inner Self, a therapist asks that Self to *describe* what it needs. Like one person asking another person what they need, they share information and build mutual trust that leads to deeper and more accurate information about needs. This line of research offers definite advantages to psychology in fostering personal growth.

Inner Selves develop within the context of a personality sponsored by Soul that promotes the development of Selves. Our research shows that a new Basic Self in a new personality often feels at risk and isolates for safety. Through its interactions with other Inner Selves, she/he gradually, over the course of many lifetimes, engages in a progression of interactions with other Selves, especially the other Basic Self.

At first, a Basic Self may be preoccupied with itself, acting only in terms of its own Self-interest as if its needs and desires seem more important than those of other Selves. In a state of *alienation*, a single Basic Self can be described as selfish, narcissistic, and unaware of the reality of the other Basic Self. Its perspective is very limited, and it assumes that it must focus on survival, even if that means harming other Selves.

As its awareness and competence expands, a single Basic Self may become fearful of losing control to its companion, turning the relationship into a power struggle that produces a state of *conflict*. When its fears subside, their relationship may settle into a state of *competition* where Basic Selves begin to work for common interests, but still conflict over priorities and role boundaries. Eventually Basic Selves learn to trust each other, resolve negative emotions and conflicts, release selfish desires, negotiate agreements, and achieve a state of *cooperation* with each other. These stages of relationship progression take place over several lifetimes.

A Basic Self advances from a state of alienation to *co-existence* to the degree that it learns how to overcome its fears. In a state of co-existence, a Self accepts the presence and needs of another Self, yet its fear limits its willingness to risk greater interaction, so it prefers to move in parallel with another Self. Long periods of time are spent in a state of co-existence.

Eventually, the two Selves encounter a clash of difference intentions, and they engage in *conflict* by attempting to impose their intentions on the other Self. The other Self resists, and they struggle in a battle of wills and competence to achieve domination through competition. Such efforts prove unstable and disagreeable as each Self seeks to become more powerful than the other.

A Basic Self learns to recognize and value the consequences of conflict that are reflected in the personality damaged by the battle. The personality might be harmed in terms of physical health, emotional instability, confused and even delusional thinking, and a lack of spiritual wellbeing and growth. Consequently, a Basic Self develops skills for resolving conflict through respect and appreciation of the other Basic Self, leading to mutual *cooperation*.

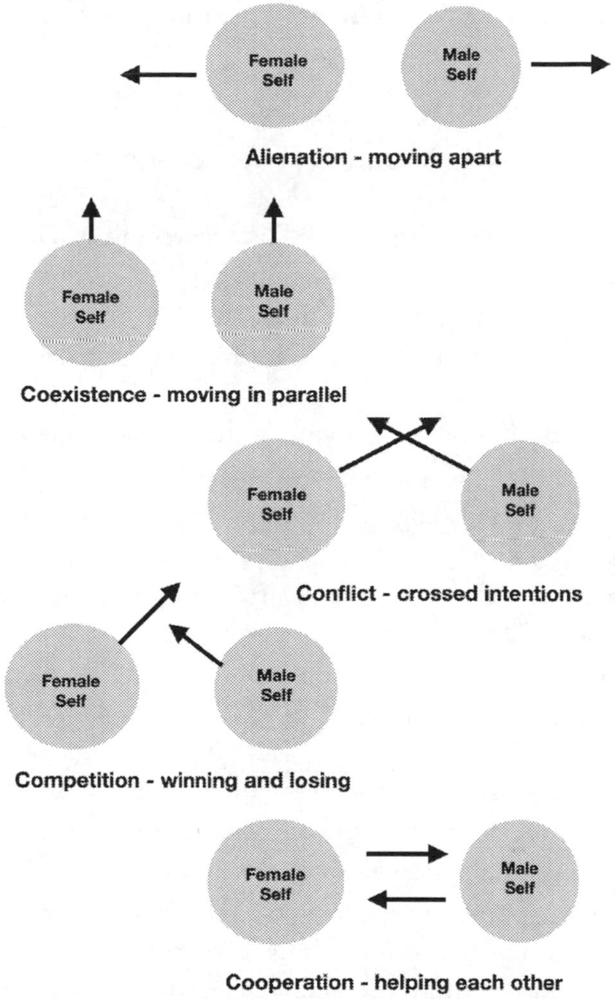

Figure 6. Basic Self Relationship Stages

However, some Basic Selves feel a need to appear better than their partners. They feel motivated to demonstrate their superiority through competition. Eventually, a Basic Self realizes that its need to outcompete arises from its feeling of inferiority, and he/she learns how to clear the limiting beliefs that suggest inferiority.

With a greater acceptance of its characteristics, a Basic Self then learns how to cooperate with its companion, beginning with mutual goals and developing into deeper levels of trust, intimacy, and love.

Figure 6 presents the stages of relationship progression into a healthy, mature relationship of Basic Selves. Other Inner Selves follow a similar progression.

Styles of Universal Consciousness

One of the most intriguing aspects of Basic Selves involves *their* awareness of their characteristics. They often report that they relate to other species than the human species. Thus far in the research, Basic Selves relate to four distinct styles of organization of consciousness related to other species:

1. **Elemental** – beings evolving through the mineral, vegetable, animal, and human kingdoms of Earth.
2. **Devic** – beings engaged in creative expression through nature and art.
3. **Outerspacial** – conceptually thinking beings related to other planets and star systems.
4. **Angelic** – beings individuated from universal consciousness attuned to Divine Will.

This finding suggests that the human species is related to its environment through the structure of universal consciousness, not merely through sharing the physical biosphere of Earth. Mystics of all ages have affirmed this profound interconnection of all life forms, yet finding more specific relationships between the human subconscious mind and other life forms may be a significant step toward greater ecological awareness.

The human species is related to its environment through the structure of universal consciousness, not merely through sharing the physical biosphere of Earth.

A person who works well with animals might have an *elemental* Basic Self who can communicate telepathically with animals. The ability of a Native American shaman to contact the spirit of the clouds to call forth rain during a drought, might be explained as the ability of an Outer Self to motivate a *devic* Basic Self to contact the deva of the clouds.

A scientist with great conceptual ability might have an *outerspacial* Basic Self. A selflessly giving person, working to help the homeless in the slums, might have an *angelic* Basic Self.

One might reasonably contend that these so-called "species" are merely symbolic representations or metaphors, and not literal species. If this contention is true, then Basic Selves may be considered as *personality styles of the subconscious* mind. Until clear evidence is gained of other species, such as elementals, devas, outerspacial beings and angels, this issue remains a matter of personal preference. Many people involved in metaphysics feel they have evidence for the existence of other species, yet most people involved in mainstream psychology do not yet recognize that evidence.

Whether Basic Self qualities represent psychological styles or actual relationships to other species does not affect the ability of an Outer Self to communicate with and understand them. On a practical basis, knowing the *style* of a Basic Self offers the Outer Self valuable clues for communicating, motivating, and cooperating with a Basic Self. The following descriptions are derived from personal explorations conducted by a group of nearly a thousand persons asking questions of their Basic Selves and observing them inwardly.

Elemental Basic Selves

Qualities:

- Elemental Basic Selves relate easily with minerals, vegetables, and animals, since they express connection with the elemental consciousness that has evolved through these Earth kingdoms of life.
- They integrate archetypal patterns in their consciousness to a degree not often found in other species, giving them a quality of unshakable stability when they are more highly evolved.
- They focus mainly on particulars, specific objects, and events.
- Their thinking is based on concrete sensory observations.
- They often do not generalize from specifics to classes of objects and events.

- They need to learn how to perform symbolic or conceptual thinking.
- They often get stuck on particulars and don't see connections.
- They have strong feelings and emotions that often overshadow their thinking.
- Their strong feelings are often related to particular objects or events.
- They are grounded in their beliefs, tending to be conservative, tenacious, and loyal.
- They are attuned to seasonal changes and natural events, responding to cycles of nature.
- Wealth and "creature comforts" are important to them.
- Their basic needs (food, home, clothes, sex, etc.) must be met for them to feel secure.
- They retreat when threatened, but will fight fiercely when provoked and cornered.
- They are very aware of their sensory input and often provide kinesthetic self-stimulation by moving their bodies.
- They tend to gesture constantly while talking.
- They prefer the outdoors to remaining inside.
- They strongly desire to belong, yet at times want to be alone.

How to Relate to Them:

- Praise them, touch them, love them.
- Be alert to their stress and fear levels when you approach them so that you don't get "bitten."
- Point them in the right direction, seek their cooperation, and don't force or order them to get things done.

How They Are Threatened:

- When they feel they have been disloyal or wrong.
- When they feel they may lose basic needs.
- When they feel abused or neglected.

Devic Basic Selves

Qualities:

- They relate easily to the dynamic and esthetic forces of nature since they express connection with the devic species that plays a creative role throughout the universe.
- They need to be creatively expressive in some way, or else they feel trapped or caged.
- If they do not feel free to express creativity, they will seek escape from confining conditions.
- They have inter-dimensional awareness and know that other dimensions are available when they feel blocked in any dimension.
- If their escape is blocked, they may become aggressive toward others as well as self-destructive.
- They may tend toward suicidal thinking when chronically frustrated.
- They are very aware of patterns as perceived in sensory input, emotions and thinking.
- They make decisions based on esthetics, seeking harmony or contrast.
- They resist conceptual or rational thinking, preferring to live in the moment.
- Their feelings are related to the context or conditions in which they live.
- They often need to be the center of attention.
- They can be impatient, arrogant, and disdainful of human beings.
- They are bored with repetition, preferring change and dramatic effects.
- They tend toward addictions as a means of escape, especially if frustrated.
- They alternate between expressions of strength and gentleness.
- They are powerful, yet need creative focus and closure.

How to Relate to Them:

- Give them opportunities to be dramatic and the center of attention.
- Above all, give them freedom of choice.
- Play with them, be spontaneous.
- Involve them in creative projects.
- Give them slack and space – generous boundaries.
- Do not order them around.
- Do not ask them to do rote work.
- Help them come to closure, pull down the curtain.

How They Are Threatened:

- When they fear loss of freedom.
- When they fear being confined, trapped, or caged.
- When they feel burdened with detailed or long-term projects.

Outerspacial Basic Selves

Qualities:

- They easily relate to conceptual plans and systems, since they claim connection with a variety of other species which have evolved on other planets and solar systems which they consider as more mentally developed than human beings.
- They want to learn and assist in accomplishing plans for spiritual growth for human beings.
- They need to learn how to be "human," how to receive and share personal love.
- They are mentally oriented, impersonal, and can often be intolerant.
- They relate more to universal principles than to personalities or situations.
- They rely greatly upon conceptual frameworks, plans, schedules, lists and budgets.
- They tend to be perfectionists, compelled to achieve higher standards and fit all the details into proper categories.

- They have a clear concept of an issue, and other people's opinions may not matter to them.
- They enjoy computers and complex machines.
- They range from being mechanical and legalistic to being highly intuitive and holistic.
- They have little awareness of emotions and often deny or avoid them, preferring to rationalize.
- When emotions arise in themselves or in others, they tend to retreat.
- They need to have emotions and associated body sensations explained to them explicitly.
- They need to share their information; if unable to do so, they will either withdraw or become aggressive.
- They tend to be precise and task-oriented in managing money, time, and resources.

How to Relate to Them:

- Explain things in factual terms that relate to concepts.
- Ask them to develop a plan for accomplishing priorities.
- Give them time to think.
- Help them through their emotions.
- Teach them communication skills, especially for communicating their emotions.
- Reveal emotions to them gradually, with explanations of the emotions since they retreat from emotional outbursts.
- Persuade them by reasoning and negotiation; don't give them orders or emotional appeals.

How They Are Threatened:

- When they think they have made a mistake.
- When they think they have messed up their plans.
- When they get off schedule, off budget, or distracted from principles.
- When they think they are trapped on Earth.

Angelic Basic Selves

Qualities:

- They relate easily to Divine Will, since they claim connection with the Angelic species of universal beings who are attuned and responsive to Divine Will.
- They act as conveyers of Divine Grace, associated with the Golden Light that assists us in learning our karmic lessons.
- They respond instantly to what they sense as Divine Will through intuitive "knowing."
- They have difficulty at first with selfhood since they identify more as universal impulses than as Selves.
- They tend to be highly empathic and compassionate.
- They tend to be Self-sacrificing, easily becoming codependents and rescuers for persons suffering from addictions.
- They have a strong sense of ethics, with an impersonal sense of justice applied equally to all persons.
- They trust others and, if they lack discernment of character, can be gullible and easily victimized.
- They easily assume the role of victim, preferring to absorb the pain themselves instead of confronting their victimizers.
- They need to learn how to set and maintain personal boundaries with assertive behavior, and how to say "No."
- They can strike out in righteous anger for the underdog.
- When they defend themselves or others, they bleed with their opponent.
- They have difficulty with limitations of time, space, and money, which they assume to be unlimited resources for all.
- They need to learn how to plan, budget, and set priorities.
- Their esthetic sense is more intense and multi-layered than the esthetic sense of devic Basic Selves.
- They are task-oriented and hard workers, finding joy in the fulfillment of work.
- Even their play has purpose in serving the greater good.

How to Relate to Them:

- Appeal to their heart and their need to serve others.
- Offer them love and service because they need it too, but often won't ask for it.
- Give them praise because they won't seek it.
- Provide them with leeway in schedules because they will tend to be late.
- Encourage them to set priorities, make plans, and follow budgets.
- Listen to what they intuitively "know" because they will probably be right, even if they can't explain it.

How They Are Threatened:

- When they feel they have hurt someone.
- When they feel unworthy to serve others.
- When they feel that they did not serve well enough.
- When they feel that they did not obey Divine Will.

Blends of Styles

In addition to these four distinct types of Basic Selves, we have discovered Basic Selves who appear to be *blends* of different styles. For example, a female Basic Self might be a blend of elemental and angelic styles, sharing those characteristics on either a *constant* or *episodic* basis. If *constant*, she behaves with combined elemental and angelic qualities all the time. If *episodic*, she behaves like an elemental part of the time and like an angel part of the time, switching from style to style to a noticeable degree. Being aware of the styles of our Basic Selves enables us to be more effective in daily living because we can meet our inner needs more specifically.

Being aware of the styles of our Basic Selves
enables us to be more effective in daily living, because
we can meet our inner needs more specifically.

Dominant and Recessive Styles

We assume that all these styles are present in us to some degree, yet some styles appear *dominant* and some *recessive* in their expression. A computer technician with strong outerspacial characteristics might enjoy occasional nature hikes to supply her more recessive elemental needs. Or, the overworked social worker with pronounced angelic qualities might seek relaxation and renewal of her devic needs by attending the opera. Both dominant and recessive styles require attention to maintain or improve balance of expression.

These characteristics have many practical uses in gaining a deeper understanding of the subconscious mind and how it may be applied productively to improve our lives.

Balance of Expression

A balanced expression of sexual polarities and styles of Basic Selves plays an important part in personal growth. As we assess the qualities of our Basic Selves, we can easily identify balances and imbalances in their expression. The Personal Self Integration method provides us with several effective tools for correcting imbalances.

If one Basic Self seems dominant and the other recessive, we can dialogue with them to arrive at an *understanding* of what will assist them to balance their expression. Once we share an understanding, we can enter a process of *negotiation* that provides incentive for each Basic Self to change its expression.

We assist our Basic Selves in resolving fears and doubts which affect their Self-esteem and level of competence. We can offer encouragement and *reinforcement* for their efforts toward positive change.

If a male Basic Self seems prejudiced against the female Basic Self and seeks to dominate or exclude her, we can follow a process for *conflict resolution* which gives them more peaceful and constructive options for meeting their respective needs. The same holds true for resolving conflicts between Basic Selves of different styles, such as an outerspacial male Basic Self who is sometimes intolerant of the angelic female Basic Self's need for having a love relationship.

---

*Knowing our Basic Selves in greater depth enables
us to work through long-term, chronic problems.*

If a Basic Self stubbornly resists change that would benefit the whole personality, we can ask it to consult with the High Self, which is more capable than the Outer Self of convincing an intransigent Basic Self to cooperate. Indeed, by dialoguing with the Basic Selves of the subconscious mind, we gain greater access to the High Self of the superconscious mind and its tremendous capabilities.

Knowing our Basic Selves in greater depth enables us to work through long-term, chronic problems in our lives by utilizing our inner intelligence effectively. Furthermore, as we cooperate more fully with our Basic Selves in mastering the lessons of our karmic plan, we gain consistent and dependable access to the wisdom of our High Self, which further empowers us in daily living.

Split Basic Selves

As we meet a Basic Self in a guided imagery process, that Self appears to be a total Basic Self. However, after a period of day, weeks, or months of getting to know that Self, we might discover that it is just one *aspect* of a Male or Female Self. For example, another aspect of a Male Self may spontaneously enter a dialogue with the Outer Self, needing to express its viewpoint that may contradict the view of the aspect that has already been communicating. The new aspect wants to be included in the relationship with the Outer Self.

In this situation, the Outer Self can ask the High Self to confirm that the new aspect is indeed a split-off aspect of the Self that was first met. In our research into this situation, we have found that the total Self encountered a traumatic event in a past life that caused the Self to split in two. For example, a Female Self in a past life experienced the trauma of a violent rape. She generated two strong reactions, one of passivity and one of aggression. Her divided reactions were sufficiently powerful to split the identity of the Female Self. One aspect identified with a passive response, and the other aspect identified with an aggressive response. Those divided responses produced two identities of the one Female Self.

In Personal Self Integration, we recognize that each aspect of a split-Self needs to follow its own course of spiritual growth until it desires to re-unite with the other aspect. A therapist needs to assist each aspect in sharing its values and priorities with the other aspect. For example in the case above, the passive aspect of a Female Self may express *angelic* consciousness while the aggressive aspect may express *elemental* consciousness. Our research has found that most cases of split-Selves involve splitting along the lines of different styles of consciousness.

A PSI therapist can identify those styles of consciousness in interviews with each aspect by using the characteristics listed in the Styles of Consciousness section of this book.

When each aspect of a split-Self is willing to unify with the other aspect, they need to develop the skills of cooperation and collaboration in assisting one another. They need to shift their values from opposition to each other into caring and serving the needs of the other. They need to resolve their deep-seated fears and demonstrate increased awareness and acceptance of the other aspect. Their efforts in achieving unification as a total Self produce mutual trust that results in a synchronization of values and priorities, flexibility in reactions, and blending of their styles of consciousness. The result of their reunification produces a wiser, more capable Self.

We note that the three other Subconscious Selves – Mental and Astral Judge Selves and the Body Self – might also appear in a split-Self configuration. Their reunification process runs in parallel with the reunification process for Basic Selves.

Basic Selves and Sub-Personalities

Unlike other counseling methods which treat Inner Selves as simplistic fragments of personality, Personal Self Integration finds that Basic Selves appear at least as intelligent and capable as Outer Selves. In fact, Basic Selves provide evidence of awareness and capability beyond the range of Outer Selves. This difference derives from the greater longevity of

Basic Selves, which exist and evolve through a long series of lifetimes, as compared to the one lifetime existence of the Outer Self.

Basic Selves provide evidence of awareness
and capability beyond the range of Outer Selves.

Personal Self Integration distinguishes between Basic Selves and "sub-personalities." Sub-personalities lack the depth, complexity, and impact of Basic Selves. While we may have sub-personalities organized around childhood experiences, such as the "hurt child within" or past life experiences of trauma or greatness, our Basic Selves exhibit a greater intelligence, psychological complexity, and ability to affect physical, emotional, and mental conditions.

Our dialogue with Basic Selves does *not* exclude work with sub-personalities; in fact, Basic Selves can help sub-personalities resolve their issues and integrate with the personality. Sub-personalities, if they are capable and willing, can also help Basic Selves with their issues, yet Basic Selves act more like "parents" and sub-personalities act more like "children" in capability.

As the process of Personal Self Integration progresses, sub-personalities tend to be "absorbed" by Basic Selves. Their need diminishes for separate, independent expressions of a trauma (negative aspect) or a talent (positive aspect), as a sub-personality is incorporated into a Basic Self.

These findings of clinical practice seem to fit the theoretical view of Basic Selves as long-term vehicles for spiritual growth. Once a Basic Self recognizes and accepts a trauma as part of its karmic lesson plan, the separate expression of a sub-personality is no longer needed. In a similar way, a sub-personality, which reminds the Basic Self of a talent or strength it previously developed in a past life, is no longer required as a separate voice once a Basic Self acknowledges and acts upon the reminder.

RESPONSIBILITIES OF BASIC SELVES

Guthrie and Karish's research suggests that Basic Selves are assigned specific responsibilities by the High Self. The High Self assigns a responsibility to a Basic Self so that it may learn to develop awareness and skills in that area of responsibility. As a Basic Self gains mastery in one area, it is assigned to another area for expansion of its capability. In some instances, only one Basic Self is placed in charge of an area because it needs to gain mastery of it. In other instances, both Basic Selves share responsibility for one area because they need to learn how to cooperate in that area.

Care of the Physical Body

Physical health is viewed by the Personal Self Integration approach as being dependent upon three factors:

1. Following the karmic plan.
2. The capability of an assigned Basic Self or Selves.
3. The quality of cooperation among Basic Selves and the Outer Self.

These factors interact and should be investigated when a person seeks healing of persistent physical health problems.

Many physical problems and illnesses represent opportunities for spiritual growth through the karmic plan of an individual. In many cases, unresolved negative emotions appear to cause physical imbalances that accumulate to create illness or physical deformity.

Doubt, fear, hatred, resentment, anger, guilt, and shame contribute to physical dysfunctions. If the Outer Self or Basic Selves fail to resolve intense emotional energies, those energies create physical problems. In such cases, the Outer Self and/or Basic Selves may need to learn how to resolve negative emotions and release those toxic energies from interacting with the physical body. For example, cancer patients can achieve significant healing from release of accumulated fears, angers, and hurts through counseling and various forms of psychotherapy and spiritual counseling.

In other cases, a physical difficulty or deformity may be used by the High Self as a means for creating conditions needed to stimulate learning on the part of a Basic Self. For example, an intolerant and impatient outerspacial Basic Self may be placed by the High Self in a physical body with cerebral palsy to learn compassion and patience.

Some physical difficulties apparently do *not* arise from karmic need, but rather from the lack of capability of a Basic Self learning the rudiments of caring for the physical body. Inexperienced Basic Selves can be assisted in their learning by obtaining either the help of a more experienced Basic Self or the instruction of a Spirit Teacher. Either option requires approval by the High Self. In any event, an inexperienced Basic Self needs to learn how to be capable of caring for the physical body.

---

*An inexperienced Basic Self needs to learn how
to be capable of caring for the physical body.*

Other physical difficulties seem to arise from alienation, co-existence, conflict, or competition between Basic Selves, or from an Outer Self who ignores the advice of its Basic Selves and overindulges in harmful behavior. In the case of disharmony between Basic Selves, an Outer Self can assist them in clarifying and resolving issues that lead to physical problems. In the case of an overindulgent Outer Self, the Basic Selves might need to allow physical problems to develop severity of symptoms sufficient to motivate the Outer Self toward greater self-discipline.

Care of Emotions

Emotional health and wellbeing depend upon the same set of factors that affect physical health. The same types of corrective steps can be taken to bring about balance of the emotions, or what might be termed the "emotional body." If a Basic Self is competent, fulfilling its part in the karmic plan and cooperating with the other Basic Self and the Outer Self, then emotional health naturally results. It properly processes negative emotions, resolves conflicts, and releases associated negative emotions so that positive emotions can prevail. If a Basic Self is incompetent or in disharmony with the other Basic Self or the Outer Self, emotional problems can accumulate to harmful levels.

The emotional body needs to be cleared, cleansed
and restored to balance practically on a daily basis.

Because the karmic plan creates a succession of stressful events in our lives, the emotional body needs to be cleared, cleansed, and restored to balance practically on a daily basis, to prevent accumulation of toxic emotional energies. An Outer Self can encourage and assist the Basic Self in charge of emotions to keep the emotional body cleared of accumulated stresses.

Care of the Chakras (Psychic Doors)

The term *chakra* derives from ancient Sanskrit and means "wheel," which describes whirling vortices of life energy distributed throughout the body. These energy centers act as gateways of vital forces entering, circulating through, and exiting the physical body. Heightened awareness and illumination can enter through these psychic doors, as can negative energies. The Basic Self entrusted with responsibility for the chakras needs to be capable of discerning and screening the entry of energies.

If a Basic Self is not fully competent, negative energies
can penetrate the bioenergetic field to influence, attack,
or even attempt to take over the personality.

If a Basic Self is competent at this job, the bioenergetic field of a person is properly maintained and protected. If a Basic Self is not fully competent, negative energies can penetrate the bioenergetic field to influence, attack, and even attempt to take over the personality. Such attempts are described as cases of obsession or possession. A Basic Self responsible for protection must learn how to detect the presence of attacking, corrosive, or parasitic energies and give warning to the other Basic Self and the Outer Self.

Once a Basic Self has gained competence in providing adequate protection, it learns how to respond to the karmic plan in opening the chakra system to higher, more beneficial and spiritual energies, thus contributing greatly to the enlightenment of the personality.

As that Basic Self learns these skills, its next step involves asking the High Self to provide protection, cleansing, and healing any harm from psychic attacks. The High Self, as a Solar Angel, has more than enough power and beneficial intentions to block and stop any level of psychic attack, even by black magicians. The Basic Self in charge of maintaining energetic balance and clarity of the personality learns how to collaborate with the High Self, observing and learning specific skills for energetic management.

Care of the Intuition

Intuition represents a vital aspect of communication among the Outer Self, Basic Selves, High Self, and even more highly evolved levels of consciousness. Intuition may be viewed as *communication of the whole being* with a single aspect of the being. Thus, a Basic Self may receive a communication of insight from the whole being relayed through the High Self. In addition to being receptive to intuitive communication, at least one Basic Self needs to relay appropriate intuitive communication to the Outer Self.

Intuition may be viewed as communication of the whole being with a single aspect of the being.

When one Basic Self gains competence in maintaining and utilizing the channels of intuition, an Outer Self begins to experience more continuous, high-quality communication with Basic Selves and High Self. If both Basic

Selves willingly participate in the intuitive process, the Outer Self benefits greatly. Until Basic Self intuitive competence is achieved, the Outer Self tends to feel isolated.

Most persons experience intuition in brief flashes, yet those flashes of intuition convey very clear messages that express the highly integrated quality of Higher Consciousness. As Basic Selves participate more completely in the intuitive communication process, they gain a greater sense of connectedness with Higher Consciousness. The intuitive process encourages them in their actions and stimulates greater Self-esteem within their being. The same holds true for Outer Selves. As an individual Self becomes capable of maintaining more continuous communication with the whole being, it becomes more secure and better able to accept its own place in the development of the whole being.

Care of Psychic Sensitivity

An Outer Self is often influenced by sensing positive, neutral, and negative energies in its environment. The Basic Self responsible for registering such impressions needs to be able to interpret those energies as *internal* (inside the personality) or *external* (from the environment). That Basic Self might have a bias that distorts its interpretation, for example, attributing an internal negative energy to the environment when it comes from another Self. This misinterpretation often occurs when a Basic Self wishes to deny the influence of the Mental Judge Self. Or on the opposite side, a Basic Self may blame the other Basic Self for negativity when that energy arises from the Astral Judge Self.

A sensitive Basic Self with low Self-esteem might be afraid of making a mistake, so it chooses not to inform the Outer Self of negative energy that might pose a threat. Also, a fearful Basic Self may confuse its fears with external negative energies and create a state of stress in the personality that is not recognized and therefore sustained. False attribution to curses, psychic attacks, astral parasites, and attempts of obsession and possession by entities might occur.

Psychic hygiene for a personality requires self-awareness and a check-and-balance routine by the responsible Basic Self to avoid creation of under-sensitivity (numbness) or hyper-sensitivity. When a Basic Self is willing to collaborate with the High Self, the High Self can demonstrate those skills for the Basic Self to learn, utilize, and develop competence.

Care of Memory

A Basic Self is also responsible for memory, including past and present lives. These memories are recalled as the Basic Self attunes to appropriate places in the Akashic Records. The Basic Self exercises memory functions, including: 1) Recall for the Outer Self; and 2) Playback of memory patterns for karmic processing of Subconscious Selves.

When an Outer Self wishes to recall a memory, the assigned Basic Self brings the memory to the Outer Self. When the High Self communicates the next step of the karmic plan to the Basic Self, that Basic Self plays back the vibrational qualities of the unresolved past life situation that presents the lesson to be learned. In some cases, the Outer Self experiences what might be called "repeat performances" of life situations until the karmic lesson is learned.

When an Outer Self wishes to recall a memory, the assigned Basic Self brings the memory to the Outer Self.

If the assigned Basic Self is competent, the Outer Self enjoys a good memory. But if the assigned Basic Self is incompetent or in disharmony with the other Basic Self or the Outer Self, memory recall may deteriorate. In such cases, the Outer Self can encourage improvement in the Basic Self's competence, ascertain what problems need fixing, and facilitate resolution of the problems underlying poor memory recall with the assistance of the High Self.

In development of dementia in mild and severe forms, the Basic Self either finds physical brain dysfunction that blocks the flow of memory to the Outer Self, or it succumbs to fear that it will be negatively judged by its shortcomings and fails to perform its job of maintaining memory. In either case, the Outer Self may ask the High Self for healing. And if the Outer Self is no longer able to make that request, one or both Basic Selves can be requested to do so on behalf of the Outer Self.

BENEFITS OF BASIC SELF DIALOGUE

Through mutual respect, caring and cooperation, the integration of Basic Selves produces:

- better physical health,
- emotional wellbeing,
- expanded sensitivity of psychic/spiritual dimensions,
- improved memory, and
- a more coherent and creative life.

Because cooperation among Outer and Basic Selves is fundamental to general wellbeing, the term **Basic Self** reminds us that this aspect of our being represents a *base* or foundation for achievement of our human potential.

Other benefits of Personal Self Integration include:

- improved spiritual connection with God,
- consistently high-quality inner guidance,
- improved interpersonal relationships, and
- development of talents and career potentials.

The following section describes some of the practical results that persons have achieved through Personal Self Integration.

CASE EXAMPLES

The following case examples, from the practice of Julie Jerrell Grady and myself, reflect actual events, and only names and some characteristics have been changed to preserve confidentiality. Only a few cases out of hundreds are presented to illustrate effects achieved by individuals working with their Basic Selves.

Healing a Cut Hand

"Damn!" Jerry cut his right hand while washing dishes. The deep cut required five stitches and didn't heal for several weeks, much to his consternation. It interfered with his ability to use his right hand, which he needed for his artwork. He looked despondent, sitting in my office holding up his bandaged hand after having tried several medications to no avail. When I suggested that the delayed healing might be caused by one of his Basic Selves, he was intrigued.

Although Jerry enjoyed good communication with his Female Basic Self, communication with his Male Basic Self, Bala, had lagged. He thought of Bala as childlike, primitive, and less interesting than the Female Basic Self. Sensing that Bala wanted more recognition and realizing that Bala exercised responsibility for physical health, I asked Jerry to talk with him. Jerry was willing. When they talked via inner dialogue, Bala said that he felt excluded by Jerry. Bala stated that he was sorry about hurting the hand, but it had seemed a good way to show Jerry his pain of being rejected.

They worked out an agreement for meeting both of their needs. The cut healed completely in two days.

Jerry assured Bala that he would be included and treated like a brother. They worked out an agreement for meeting both of their needs. The cut healed completely in two days. Bala's power and capabilities were recognized and appreciated. Jerry dialogued more often with Bala, deepening their relationship. Physical problems, he learned, can be a means for stimulating deeper inner awareness which produces its own rich rewards.

Healing of Abnormal Menstrual Cycle

Esther, a businesswoman, became alarmed when her menstrual period began to occur two or three times a month, depleting her energies. After a checkup, her doctor referred her to a gynecologist who recommended a hysterectomy. Horrified, Esther tried both medical and holistic healing remedies without significant improvement.

Three months later, she came to me for counseling. Since her personal and work lives were otherwise in good order, I thought the cause probably came from the subconscious level. I introduced her to her Female Basic Self, Aruna, who told Esther that she, Aruna, had caused the physical problem as a desperate measure to get Esther to listen to her. Aruna explained that Esther's lifestyle contained too much work and not enough creative expression, which caused her psychic ability to operate at a trickle. Aruna warned that the physical problem would persist until Esther met these needs.

Surprised at this outburst and at the intensity expressed by Aruna, Esther promised that she would provide more creative expression. Only when it happened, Aruna stated, would she relax her hold on Esther's body. Esther wanted results now, but Aruna held firm. So Esther went into action. She rearranged her schedule and renewed some artistic expression that she had not done in more than a year. Aruna kept her word, and Esther's physical problems ceased in one week.

Aruna kept her word, and Esther's physical problems
ceased in one week.

Overcoming Shame in a Career Choice

Henry desperately wanted to be a musician, but felt shame at the thought of exploring the possibility. He ran a small business and was his own boss, yet something inside kept persuading him to "be responsible" by sticking to his job and not be tempted by frivolity. Henry obeyed this inner voice for years, but felt more heartsick as time went by. With counseling, he discovered that his Male Basic Self, George, needed the security of a plan. To George, becoming a musician was like stepping into quicksand, so he resisted Henry's longings.

Henry realized that a more effective approach to gaining George's cooperation involved creating a phase-by-phase plan for exploring a career in music without abandoning his business. He worked out a plan with George, and George agreed to support it. Starting music lessons would be the first step. George agreed that the cost was reasonable.

Henry found his chronic years-long depression lifting, as he experimented first with music lessons and then playing in a small band. George became interested in the logical structure of music, a role that allowed him to participate. Benefitting from inner support, Henry no longer felt shamed about being a musician. He also consulted George in management of the business so that George could easily express any concerns. By meeting George's needs, Henry was successfully able to pursue his own.

---

*By meeting George's needs, Henry was
successfully able to pursue his own.*

Overcoming the Paralysis of Fear

Despite fear knotted in her stomach, Shelly could have handled the news of her breast cancer and pending surgery if it hadn't been for her finances. She crumpled the paper and dropped her pencil on the desk. Juggling figures did not change the fact that her clerical job could not cover her expenses now. She must return home and live again with her abusive father.

The moment Shelly entered her parents' house, it seemed as if she had never left. All the old feelings of helplessness and fear washed over her. She felt like a powerless victim. Under her father's ceaseless attack, Shelly became increasingly depressed. She held to her clerical work grimly, sensing the threat of losing her job due to poor performance. Her self-image deteriorated, and her unhappiness grew in the months following. She became chronically anxious. Even though she was physically healthy and able to afford it, Shelly could not bring herself to leave home. Finally she found the courage to seek help.

She sought the counseling of Julie Jerrell Grady. She had been home more than a year, she told Julie. She felt paralyzed about her situation and powerless to change it. Julie helped her identify her fears and discover where they were unrealistic. Shelly remained in her state of emotional paralysis for two more months. Then Julie introduced Shelly to her Basic Selves.

Shelly's angelic Female Basic Self
was the cause of the paralysis.

They discovered that Katrina, Shelly's angelic Female Basic Self, was the cause of the paralysis. Her image of Katrina was that of a hurt little girl who wanted to stay shivering in a closet in preference to venturing out into a threatening world. With guidance from Julie, Shelly gradually convinced Katrina that she could be supported by the Male Basic Self, Ken, whose image was that of a capable man. But Katrina would have to face her unrealistic fears head on. Both Katrina and Shelly asked Ken to help, and he assured them he would.

Katrina agreed to accept a move into independent living. Shelly leased an apartment. She asked Ken to help her improve her job performance, and her performance did improve. Shelly's sense of wellbeing increased tremendously when she was given a promotion. Katrina's trust of Ken's support grew swiftly, while Shelly's fears diminished and her confidence solidified. Before long, Shelly found a man who was interested in her. She began to explore the relationship with a freedom she had never experienced. Shelly's life had turned around because of her newfound Basic Selves. "Best of all," she said beaming at Julie, "I will always have them with me."

Overcoming Deep Fear "White-Outs"

"I don't know what to do," Amy sobbed, drying tears from her face. "I just can't control it." Exposed to traumas of incest during childhood and a self-righteous, critical father, Amy frequently experienced "white-outs" when she lost orientation and ability to function in certain ways. One way involved her mathematical ability, where she would sometimes be unable, as an adult, to add or subtract her checkbook. Also, in situations like childhood experiences of shaming by her father, she would freeze at the thought of confronting someone or of asserting her own viewpoint in a conversation. "When I even think of stating *my* opinion, my mind goes blank. I can't develop a real friendship. Nobody really knows me."

In counseling, Amy discovered that her angelic Female Basic Self, Dora, felt like a sacrificial victim. Dora felt powerless in many situations, especially when she was cued into traumatic memories or when she faced possible criticism from a man. Amy's outerspacial Male Basic Self, Sol, seemed distant and unreliable. When Amy took the time to know Sol better, she found that he *was* reliable, but that she had kept him distant out of fear. Her traumatic experiences with her father had made her fearful of males in any form. Julie suggested that she encourage a supportive relationship between Sol and Dora so that Dora could ask Sol to help her when she felt powerless.

Amy was uncertain at first, but began encouraging Dora and Sol to talk to each other. She held dialogues with them until they began to trust each other. Dora's timidity toward Sol mirrored Amy's fear of her father. "Why should I rely on him?," asked Dora, trying to back out of her commitment to accept help from Sol. Amy encouraged Dora to experiment with going *through* her fear instead of being stuck in it. Dora hesitantly asked Sol to help her balance her checkbook. Sol said, "Sure, just relax and let me do it for you." Both Dora and Amy were amazed when the checkbook matched the bank statement. As Dora found she could trust Sol, so did Amy.

Amy learned to ask Sol to help her in challenging situations, and he actually did. "Will you help me express myself in the Incest Survivors Association meeting?" she wondered. "I will support you, but you have to feel it and say it yourself," Sol replied. Amy wasn't sure how it would work, but she put it to the test. During the meeting Amy had the image of Sol and Dora holding hands while Amy talked about her incest experiences for the first time in a group. Afterwards, Amy felt lighter than ever before, as though she had taken off a ton of armor.

Amy had the image of Sol and Dora holding hands while Amy talked about her incest experiences for the first time in a group.

Amy's "white-out" episodes reduced significantly within a few weeks. She could handle math easily with Sol's assistance. When Amy felt anxious about asserting her viewpoint or confronting someone, she asked Sol and Dora to help her, and consequently Amy gradually gained the ability to speak and act assertively. Eventually she was able to be assertive with her father who was surprised that he could no longer dominate her. "I have never felt so free. There's a beautiful world for me to explore," Amy exclaimed, smiling and opening her arms to life.

Overcoming Suicidal Tendencies

Mamie was suicidal when she came to Julie for counseling. Coming from an abusive family, she had felt persecuted all her life. As a businesswoman, she had successfully converted her love of arts and crafts into a business that gave her a living, yet she had ungrounded suspicions that business associates were undermining her. Her love of art was based on her need for freedom of expression without dependence on anyone else. Her attempts at forming love relationships had failed, one after the other, when suspicions overcame her affections.

Julie helped Mamie identify her emotional patterns and find better options, but Mamie seemed unable to exercise those options. Although Mamie had eased off suicidal tendencies upon receiving emotional support from Julie, she still felt stuck. If she was unable to achieve a breakthrough, Mamie would likely return to suicide to end her emotional pain.

---

*When introduced to her Basic Selves, Mamie
found them both in the victim role, feeling persecuted
in this lifetime as they had been in prior lives.*

When introduced to her Basic Selves, Mamie found them both in a victim role, feeling persecuted in this lifetime as they had been in prior lives. In addition, Mamie's High Self advised that the abusive family experience in this lifetime had been intended to give incentive to the Basic Selves to break out of the victim role, but they had only achieved a measure of independence. They remained stuck in the memory pattern of being persecuted. With the High Self's guidance, relevant past lives were explored, emotional energies released, and earlier past lives with roles as persecutors revealed.

As her Basic Selves released themselves from the pattern of persecution, Mamie felt the easing of suspicions and began to experience feelings of trust, faith, and equality. She no longer needed to be someone who felt separate from and above others. Her business, which had been marginal, became more profitable and certainly more enjoyable to her. She began to approach love relationships with a new confidence. Thoughts of suicide had long since faded away.

Attracting More Clients for Business

Jackson had run his small business of technical training for several years with erratic results. His typical pattern had consisted of working in spurts, punctuated by days and sometimes weeks without any new clients. When business boomed, he did well financially, but when it lagged, he had trouble paying bills. He wondered if something might be done by his Basic Selves to make his business more consistently profitable so that he would not have to worry about bills.

Through dialogues with his Basic Selves, Jackson learned that his devic Female Basic Self, Isadora, was primarily interested in artistic expression, not business. She enjoyed having the slack time in her business for use in creating art. She was dramatic and powerfully expressive in all her actions, so she was an obvious asset in giving Jackson the skill of an excellent teacher. However, Isadora was not motivated to maintain a steady business.

Basic Selves play a major role in attracting clients for business, using their telepathic means of communication to motivate the Basic Selves of potential clients.

Through guidance, Jackson became aware that Basic Selves play a major role in attracting clients for business, using their telepathic means of communication to motivate the Basic Selves of potential clients, even when they have no conscious knowledge of the business to which they are attracted. One of the implications of this awareness was that if Isadora wanted time for artistic expression, she might discourage potential clients through her telepathic communications.

Jackson realized that he could not deny Isadora's needs for creative expression without suffering a backlash effect. He understood that he needed to re-direct Isadora's abilities by positively motivating her. He, too, enjoyed the times of artistic expression, but he knew that business should have higher priority. When business reached a certain income level, he could schedule part of his time for art. With a steady income, he would not have to waste time and energy struggling against Isadora's desires to generate new business clients.

He felt that he could motivate Isadora by promising her that he would set aside adequate time for artistic expression each week and use part of the income generated to buy new equipment she had long wanted to further her artistic explorations. Aware of her devic qualities, he carefully consulted her about these arrangements so that she felt included in the plans, not limited by them. He helped her view the plan as a creative project: if income could be boosted significantly, then in the free time available they could produce saleable art which might further boost income.

Jackson asked Isadora to attract two new clients to his business each week. In exchange for her assistance, she would have his full cooperation during artistic times and, as steady income poured in, he would buy the equipment she wanted. Jackson wondered if the plan would really work, since he intended taking no extra steps for recruitment of new clients. To his pleasant surprise, he found that an abundant number of new clients contacted him from the first week the plan went in effect. He expressed his delight to Isadora and kept his end of their agreement. One of the new clients even offered him free use of a professional studio on weekends, when he had time for art.

His income level over a period of two months was five times the monthly average of the previous year.

As the plan continued, his income level over a period of two months was **five** times the monthly average of the previous year. Several times he received more than the recruitment goal of two new clients a week. By the end of two months, all his work time was filled to capacity. He wondered whether he should use some of the time scheduled for art, but Isadora disagreed, so he maintained his commitment to her. Thus far, he has been more consistently productive in business and art than at any other time in his life.

Gaining Access to Past Lives and Writing Ability

Jenny was a very frustrated lady in her sixties with chronic back and neck pain that brought her to counseling. Her husband was dying of emphysema and required her assistance to keep him alive. Jenny was intelligent and had been a professional writer of nonfiction articles and a few books, but she had suffered from writer's block for more than ten years. She felt her writing career was over. For her, life was a daily struggle through the darkness of despair. She had been emotionally abused as a child by her family and had married a man distressingly like her father. Now her invalid husband was dying gradually, and all she could do was watch it happen.

First, I used Emo-Sensing to help Jenny release accumulations of emotional energies that kept her body stressed and painful. As her physical pain level decreased, she became more amenable to counseling. Because her skepticism about herself had solidified over sixty years, I used guided imagery methods to give her experiences beyond her normal Outer Self's experience. Although she resisted the concept of Inner Selves, she accepted the notion that she could contact a Spiritual Teacher who could show her how to open herself to new possibilities.

Through guided imagery, I introduced Jenny to a Spiritual Teacher who was convincingly real to her. He promptly advised her to examine her past lives. Although she had considered the possibility of past lives, Jenny had never to her knowledge experienced any memories of past lives. However, she was willing to explore the possibility since that might be more interesting than her present lifetime.

The Spiritual Teacher guided her through the experiences of seventeen past lives.

In subsequent weeks and months, the Spiritual Teacher guided her through the experiences of seventeen past lives. Jenny gained ability to explore by herself those lifetimes to which we had already opened access. As the karmic patterns emerged, she realized that she had attempted on several occasions to help others, but had often been rejected and frustrated. Consequently, she had adopted skepticism as emotional armoring against such hurts. She also realized that she had inappropriately blamed God for her predicaments, and that she, not God, had created her difficulties and challenges. Whether the past life memories were valid or not, the multiple lifetime perspective that she gained now enabled her to reassess her attitudes and perceptions. She began to write a book about these past lives, but bogged down before it was completed.

In her reassessment, Jenny opened to the concept of Inner Selves, and I introduced her to her Male and Female Basic Selves. She felt that her inner being had expanded to new and exciting dimensions. She found that she could relate to past lives through her Basic Selves in a way that made more sense to her than the idea that her Outer Self had lived before. She had uncovered *subconscious*, not conscious memories of past lives.

Jenny discovered that Albert, her outerspacial Male Basic Self, was more aware of past lifetimes as a man, while Gloria, her angelic Female Basic Self, was more aware of past lifetimes as a woman. She also found out that Albert and Gloria had collaborated in several of the more recent lifetimes, and that they were learning how to accept each other more completely. This understanding helped Jenny to view her demanding experiences with her father and husband in terms of Gloria's difficulties in relating to Albert.

Gloria viewed Albert as a cold, intellectual, dominating, yet needful man who was often insensitive to her needs, but who obviously needed her help. Jenny related more easily to Gloria than to Albert, so she learned more about Gloria through dialogues. She avoided knowing much about Albert, preferring to ask him to do menial things for her, such as helping her with memory. Jenny realized that the inner relationship of her Basic Selves affected her outer relationships with men.

With this realization, Jenny reinterpreted her past life memories and gained a clearer understanding of their progressive lessons. She began rewriting portions of her book to reflect this understanding, asking Albert and Gloria for more detailed past life memories. She also encouraged them to review the lessons they had learned and were still learning through the sequence of lifetimes. Jenny developed an inner "family" feeling as she and her Basic Selves grew to accept each other more fully. She found the "family" that she had previously missed.

Jenny developed an inner "family" feeling as she and her Basic Selves grew to accept each other more fully.

Improving A Love Relationship

Louise was an attractive businesswoman in her forties who had never been able to sustain a lasting love relationship. She had no difficulty in attracting men, but for some unknown reason they preferred to leave her after a short time together. Her frustrations had caused her to consider herself unattractive or unworthy of a love relationship. Her skepticism grew with each failure.

On meeting Louise, I sensed the difficulty and asked her if she would be willing to invest a half hour in Basic Self training. She agreed, and I introduced her to her Male and Female Basic Selves. She discovered that her outerspacial Male Basic Self, Gondolph, was over-protective. He wished to be in control of her life events, and emotions such as personal love seemed to him irrelevant and distracting. Gondolph dominated the devic Female Basic Self, Sonia, most of the time, especially as Louise worked successfully in the business world. Yet Gondolph was threatened by Sonia's actions in seeking love relationships.

Sonia desperately wanted the love of a man. Her powerful emotions at first would overwhelm Gondolph's rational attempts to maintain control, then he would seize any opportunity to attack the Basic Selves of Louise's male partner. Gondolph's telepathic attacks were beyond the awareness of Louise, so she had no idea what was happening to drive men away from her. The men felt alienated and attacked by Louise, even though she had not consciously done anything of the kind. They would just leave her without explanation, leaving Louise hurt and confused.

I advised Louise to negotiate with Gondolph, informing him that she appreciated his help with her business, but that she would no longer tolerate his dominance. She entered these negotiations with my coaching, finding to her surprise that Gondolph already realized that he had been over-controlling and was missing his opportunity to experience personal love. He was willing to relate as equals with Sonia if she agreed to be more moderate with her emotions. Sonia, in turn, agreed to explain emotional energies to Gondolph so that he could participate in their expression.

Unlike the other men before him,
he did not abandon her.

As Sonia and Gondolph related more as peers, Louise tentatively accepted a man's offer to date. She was pleasantly surprised with his deepening interest in her. Unlike the other men before him, he did not abandon her. I coached Louise to maintain a daily dialogue with Gondolph and Sonia to work out any difficulties that might arise. She did so and was pleased to report at the end of a month that her date had become a boyfriend and might develop into something more. Even her business associates had commented on her new femininity, which she felt was an asset to her business.

TRAINING AVAILABLE

This brief review of cases demonstrates the promise of working with Basic Selves as both a preventive and remedial tool for a wide variety of problems. This approach enhances an individual's ability to exercise personal responsibility in overcoming her/his challenges to physical, emotional, and mental health.

Counselors and therapists should be aware that some persons will resist this approach out of fear, especially those who are in a state of denial and avoidance of their problems. Some persons will rationalize that they feel too disconcerted by thinking of themselves as "separate pieces" to try this method. In such cases, other approaches might be attempted first to reduce levels of fear, denial, and avoidance before seeking to introduce Basic Selves.

As an instructive tool for achieving human potential, working with Basic Selves offers individuals and groups some very powerful methods for teaching persons how to tap the potential of their subconscious and superconscious minds.

Interested persons are welcome to contact the Center for Human Potential for training programs in Personal Self Integration. We offer training for individuals and groups on two levels, personal training and therapist training that include working with all Inner Selves.

Personal training involves a person in meeting all relevant Inner Selves and learning how to create harmony among them. This gives a person adequate self-help skills for resolving personal problems and achieving personal goals.

Therapist training involves a person who has completed advanced experiential training for learning a variety of therapeutic skills in Personal Self Integration. These skills enable a person to conduct Personal Self Integration training with individuals and groups. Certification may be granted by the Center for Human Potential to graduates of therapist training.

REFERENCES

1   Freud, Sigmund. *An Outline of Psychoanalysis*. New York: Norton, 1949.

2   Jung, Carl G. The Collective Works of C.G. Jung. Translated by R. F. C. Hull. Princeton University Press: Bollingen Series XX, 1971.

3   Assagioli, Roberto. Psychosynthesis: A Collection of Basic Writings. New York: Penguin, Esalen Book Series, 1977.

4   Maslow, Abraham. Toward A Psychology of Being. Princeton: Van Nostrand, 1962.

5   White, John. The Highest State of Consciousness. New York: Doubleday, 1972.

6   Tart, Charles T. Transpersonal Psychologies. New York: Harper & Row, 1975.

7   Guthrie, Wayne, and Karish, Bella. Pathways to Your Three Selves. Burbank, CA: Fellowship of Universal Guidance, 1989.

8   Karish, Bella, and Miller, William. Working with Your Three Selves: Discovering and Understanding Your Purpose in Life. Juniper Springs Press, 2005.

9   Guthrie, Wayne, and Karish, Bella. Portals to Your Higher Consciousness: Exploring and Embracing Your Three Selves. Juniper Springs Press, 2018.

10 Wilber, Ken. Eye to Eye: The Quest for a New Paradigm. Boston, Massachusetts & Shaftesbury, Dorset, England: Shambhala Publications, Inc., 1990.

11 Pitstick, Mark and Schwartz, Gary E. Greater Reality Living: Integrating the Evidence for Eternal Consciousness into Your Daily Life, 2018.

12 Ed. Plante, Thomas G. and Schwartz, Gary E. Human Interaction with the Divine, The Sacred, and the Deceased: Psychological, Scientific, and Theological Perspectives. Routledge, 2022.

13 Whitefield, Charles L. Healing the Child Within: Discovery and Recovery for Adult Children of Dysfunctional Families. Deerfield Beach, FL; Health Communications, Inc., 1987.

14 Berne, Eric. Games People Play. New York: Grove Press, Inc., 1964.

15 Stone, Hal, and Winkelman, Sidra. Embracing Our Selves. Marina del Rey, CA: Devorss & Co., 1985.

16 Roberts, Susan C. "Multiple Realities: How MPD is shaking up our notions of the Self, the Body, and even the origins of evil." Common Boundary Magazine: May/June, 1992.

INDEX

Printed in the United States
by Baker & Taylor Publisher Services